LET ME SPEAK

HUMAN HORIZONS SERIES

LET ME SPEAK

by

Dorothy M. Jeffree and Roy McConkey

A CONDOR BOOK
SOUVENIR PRESS (E&A) LTD

First published 1976 by Souvenir Press Educational & Academic Ltd,
43 Great Russell Street, London WC1B 3PA

and simultaneously in Canada

Reprinted February 1978
Reprinted October 1978
Reprinted June 1979
Reprinted June 1980
Reprinted February 1982

ISBN 0 285 64828 4   casebound
ISBN 0 28 64829 2   paperback

Printed in Great Britain by
Billing & Sons Limited,
Guildford, London and Worcester

ACKNOWLEDGEMENT

Many of the games in the book were developed in the context of the Parental Involvement Project which was directed by the authors. The project was financed jointly by the Department of Health & Social Security and the Department of Education & Science, and was based at the Hester Adrian Research Centre, University of Manchester.

CONTENTS

PREFACE

This book is written primarily for parents whose children are slow in acquiring language but it should prove useful to anyone, parent or professional, who is interested in furthering any child's language development. Throughout, the emphasis is on practical suggestions for games and activities designed to help the development of language. All aspects of language development are covered, from the early stages, even before the child begins to talk, right up to the use of language in thinking.

The book is divided into four sections and parents are directed to the sections which are most applicable to their child. Hence there is no need to read the whole book at a time. Within each section there are a number of short, self-contained booklets, each dealing with a specific topic and describing a variety of teaching games. A word of warning though: throughout the book we tend to talk of the mum as the person playing the games and to refer to the child as 'he'. This is done solely for ease of reference and is no excuse for dads to leave it all to mum!

We are particularly grateful to the many parents and professionals who went to the trouble to send us their comments and ideas for games, and to their children who taught us a lot. We would also like to thank Simon Hewson for his help in preparing the book, and Janet Baldwin for typing the various manuscripts.

INTRODUCTION

PART 1: INTRODUCING LANGUAGE

The importance of language

No one in this day and age can possibly underestimate the importance of language. We are surrounded by talking, it comes to us over the radio, on the television, through the loud-speaker, at the railway station. It's used everywhere.

No wonder parents stress the importance of their children's speech. So much so that any speech delay is a source of deep concern. Rightly so, for children with speech difficulties do need extra help and early remediation.

However *all* children have had to learn to talk at one time and most have learnt at their mother's knee. Mothers are their first teachers. Indeed, they are the *best* people to teach their children to talk. Nevertheless, this task is not so easy with children whose speech is delayed or difficult. In order to help them, mothers need to know what language does entail for there is much more to language than just being able to talk.

What language entails

1. Speech is never an end in itself, it is always a means to an end. We use it to convey meaning, purpose and to bring results. To attempt to teach a child 'parrot fashion' would be to miss the point.
2. Understanding comes before the spoken word. Children understand more than they can express, as a rule. When teaching language we have, above all, to help this understanding to develop.
3. There is more to language than single words. We have to learn how to put words together to form sentences. This

is a difficult lesson but once a child has learnt it he is able to express his own ideas more freely.

4. It is difficult to imagine thinking without language. In fact we often 'think aloud'. Putting things into words helps us to remember them. Language also helps us to order our everyday tasks and to think logically.

5. Language even helps us to notice things which would otherwise pass us by. It helps children to concentrate on what they are doing without being at the mercy of every fleeting impression.

6. Through language children learn to communicate with their fellows and to be accepted by them. This means learning to listen and to take turns.

7. Children can use language to express their own feelings and aches and pains. Once these can be shared, much unhappiness and frustration can be avoided.

8. Children need to be shown that speech is both expected and worthwhile. They should not have all their desires anticipated but be shown that when they 'ask' it brings results.

9. Language learning does not stop as soon as a child can speak in sentences. Every new task requires a new vocabulary and language enters into all learning.

However, just as no child can hope to run before he can walk or crawl, so he cannot learn to speak until he has the requisite skills.

The foundations of language

These are some of the skills children need before language can develop:

1. *Sounds* – Children must be able to make a variety of sounds and make their voices rise and fall rhythmically.

2. *Hearing* – They need to be able to hear and locate sounds and attend to the important ones and ignore the others.

3. *Imitation* – They need to be able to copy actions and especially to copy sounds and sound patterns.

4. *Imagination* – Children need to be able to use their

imagination, in 'make believe'. This shows they have begun to make mental pictures of objects which are no longer present.

5. *Object Recognition* – Before naming objects a child must be able to recognise familiar objects even in strange surroundings. He shows us he can do this when he starts to look for hidden toys.

Once a child shows that he has mastered these skills you can then concentrate on language development.

Stages of language development

A child's language develops in a regular sequence of stages. For instance he coos, babbles and repeats syllables like 'Mama', before using a single word. In Part 3 we will describe how you can observe your child and find the stage he has reached in his language development. We can then direct you to the most appropriate sections of the book for ideas to help his development. You will not need to read the whole book.

Why is Mum in the best position to help her child?

Many parents seek expert help with a child who is language-delayed. However, there are not enough professionals to go round (and probably never will be) and even if 'the mum' is lucky enough to receive expert help, no professional will have time to see her child very often, so she is still left literally 'holding the baby'. We have already said that mothers are generally the child's first teachers of language. This does not mean that fathers, brothers and sisters or grandparents are excluded, for they too have an important part to play, but her child's language development will always depend more upon her than upon anyone else. She is, in many ways, the ideal person to help her child for the following reasons:

1. There is a special bond between a mother and her child. It is she who best understands his changing moods and adapts to them. This bond is formed right from birth and nobody can really take her place.

2. A child learns best from a person who spends a lot of time with him. Mum is the ideal person, for not only

does she spend a great deal of time with her child, but she always uses the same expressions and tone of voice. This is much less confusing than learning from several different people. Also children learn to speak better from grown-ups (who are 'experts' in talking) than from other children.

3.   A mother needs to spend time with her child when she is feeding, washing and dressing him etc. These caretaking activities are ideal opportunities for introducing language for then it will be meaningful and worthwhile for the child (especially at meal-time!).

4.   We say a baby learns at his mother's knee, but when it comes to language, it may be more accurate to say that he learns *on* his mother's knee. Here it is much easier for a child to pick out what his Mum says from the other noises around him. He can watch her lips more and follow her glance. This helps him to understand what the sounds mean.

Let Me Speak

Many parents may feel they have not sufficient knowledge to help their child adequately. This book is designed to give parents expertise without being too academic. There are not nearly enough language experts to go round, nor can we afford to waste time waiting for them. We have to make a start ourselves. All our suggestions are in the form of games designed to help your child's development and yet be fun at the same time. To make it easier we have divided this book into a series of booklets. You will not need to read it all.

The next part of the Introduction (Using the Book, p. 18) will tell you how to set about using the book.

However, we would like to make two suggestions, which we feel would help you to get more out of the book:

1.   *Contact other parents* – In our experience, parents can learn a lot from other parents, especially those whose children are experiencing, or have experienced, the same problems. If possible, try to contact some parents in your area –

put up a notice at the local clinic or hospital; contact voluntary societies organised by parents (see Telephone Directory) or ask at your child's nursery or school or contact your Health Visitor to see if she knows of anyone.

If a group of you can get together this will give you a chance to discuss problems together, to pick each other's brains for ideas or share useful toys, books, etc. Most of all, though, you will probably find the group a source of encouragement. There will be times when you feel you are getting nowhere, but if you can talk to somebody who had the same problem, then it won't seem as hopeless as you thought.

2. *Ask advice* – don't be afraid of asking for advice from professionals who are in contact with your child – psychologists, teachers, speech therapists etc. Tell them about the games you are using and if you encounter any problems or if you are unsure of what to do, then ask them if they have any suggestions. Indeed, we believe that the closer parents and professionals work together, then the more the child benefits.

PART 2: USING THE BOOK

In the first part of the Introduction we described what is meant by the term 'Language' and some of the skills that a child has to have in order to be able to use language to communicate with other people. In the remainder of the book we will be giving suggestions for games and activities which you can use to help your child's language development.

To make it easier we have divided the book into four sections, so there is no need to read the whole book.

If your child is not talking yet, you will probably find Section 1 (p. 39) most useful, as this deals with the foundations of language.

If your child has started to talk, even if only in single words, you will probably find Section 2 (p. 77) useful, as this deals with the development of language skills, and Section 3 (p. 119), for this is concerned with encouraging children to use language.

If your child has acquired the major language skills, e.g. talks in sentences, you could concentrate on Section 3 (p. 119) encouraging the child to use language, and Section 4 (p. 147) which deals with the use of language in thinking.

Each of the Sections 1 to 4 contains a number of short, self-contained booklets, each dealing with a specific topic. The Contents Page at the beginning of the book gives a brief description of each booklet.

You will probably find that all the booklets within a section are relevant to your child, although some may be more appropriate than others. To give you some idea of what the booklets are like, read through the section which you think is suitable for your child. You can then come back and finish reading the next two parts of the Introduction, which should be read carefully *before* you start playing the games.

Part 3: Language Development Charts (p. 20) will give you an idea of which booklets will be particularly appropriate for your child; give you a chance to observe and record the language skills your child has at present; and outline the stages children go through in learning language.

Part 4: Points to Remember (p. 36) suggests some rules to be followed during the games and activities if you are to be successful in helping your child to learn.

Finally, we would like to draw your attention to two further things:

(1) TOY AND BOOK SUPPLIERS. Throughout the book we mention particular toys, books or materials which you should use in the games. Many of these are easily made by yourself, but where suitable equipment is commercially produced we have mentioned the name of the manufacturer. At the back of the book is a list of manufacturers' addresses in case you want to contact them for catalogues, order forms etc.

(2) INDEX OF GAMES. Many of the games we recommend can be used at different stages of language learning in slightly different ways. We have done this deliberately, for once a child has grasped the basic idea of a game and enjoys playing it, then it is much easier to help him to learn new things by modifying the known game than by introducing a completely new one. If you want to see how a particular game can be developed, turn to the Index of Games at the back of the book. This gives the pages of the book where each game is described.

PART 3: LANGUAGE DEVELOPMENT CHARTS

We hope that you will find this part of the book helpful in *four* different ways. We realise that this may mean reading this part four times to get the most out of it, so if you don't feel like doing that after reading it through once go ahead to the next part of the Introduction (Points to Remember; p. 36), and even make a start on some of the games. You can always come back to this part again.

The four ways in which you should find the charts helpful are:

1. *Language development* – they describe just what is involved in language development and also outline the stages children go through in learning language.

2. *Observing your child's language* – the charts point out specific things that you can look out for in your child.

3. *Recording your child's language skills* – you will be able to record which skills your child has acquired up to the present. Later, you can look back and see how much he has progressed.

4. *Guide to booklets* – once you have filled in the charts, we can then point out which of the booklets in Sections 1 to 4 would be particularly appropriate for your child.

On pages 32 to 35 we will be discussing each of the above points; but first, have a look at the charts* to get an idea of what they are like.

---

* These charts have been taken, with some modifications, from our P.I.P. Developmental Charts, published by Hodder & Stoughton. The P.I.P. charts cover all aspects of children's development – physical, social, eye-hand and play development, as well as language development.

Chart 1: Spoken Language

Booklets

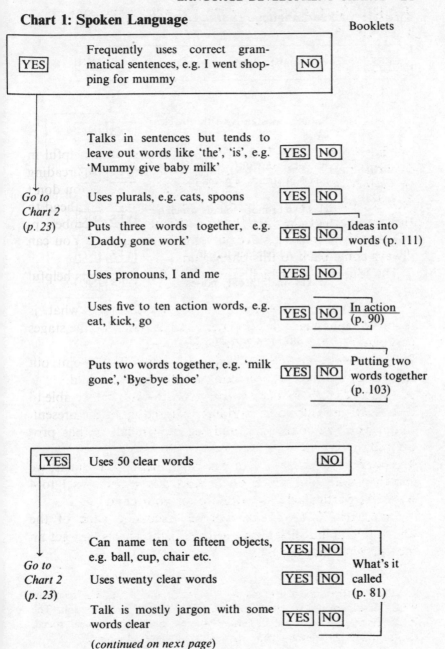

YES	Frequently uses correct grammatical sentences, e.g. I went shopping for mummy NO

Go to
Chart 2
(p. 23)

Talks in sentences but tends to leave out words like 'the', 'is', e.g. 'Mummy give baby milk'   YES   NO

Uses plurals, e.g. cats, spoons   YES   NO

Puts three words together, e.g. 'Daddy gone work'   YES   NO   Ideas into words (p. 111)

Uses pronouns, I and me   YES   NO

Uses five to ten action words, e.g. eat, kick, go   YES   NO   In action (p. 90)

Puts two words together, e.g. 'milk gone', 'Bye-bye shoe'   YES   NO   Putting two words together (p. 103)

YES	Uses 50 clear words NO

Go to
Chart 2
(p. 23)

Can name ten to fifteen objects, e.g. ball, cup, chair etc.   YES   NO

Uses twenty clear words   YES   NO   What's it called (p. 81)

Talk is mostly jargon with some words clear   YES   NO

(*continued on next page*)

Chart 1: Spoken Language *continued*

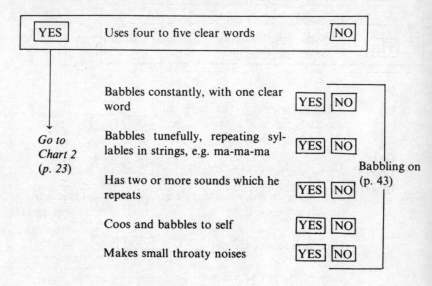

| YES | Uses four to five clear words | NO |

Go to
Chart 2
(*p. 23*)

Babbles constantly, with one clear word — YES NO

Babbles tunefully, repeating syllables in strings, e.g. ma-ma-ma — YES NO

Has two or more sounds which he repeats — YES NO

Babbling on (p. 43)

Coos and babbles to self — YES NO

Makes small throaty noises — YES NO

Go to Chart 2 (p. 23)

Chart 2: Using Language

Booklets

| YES | Continually asking questions, 'why', 'when' etc. | NO |

Go to Chart 3 (p. 24)

Describes in detail what he wants, e.g. 'chocolate cake with sweet on'   YES NO   Sorting it out (p. 156)

Carries on simple conversations about past experiences   YES NO   Talking together (p. 136) Try to Remember (p. 151)

Asks for things he wants by their name, e.g. at table says 'cake', 'milk' etc.   YES NO

Uses words to make wants known, e.g. 'Gimme', 'me' etc.   YES NO   Ask for it (p. 128)

Makes a particular noise when he wants attention   YES NO

Go to Chart 3 (p. 24)

Chart 3: Understanding Language

Booklets

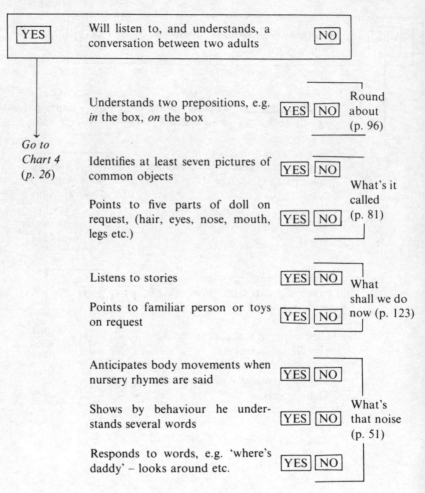

YES — Will listen to, and understands, a conversation between two adults — NO

Go to
Chart 4
(p. 26)

Understands two prepositions, e.g. *in* the box, *on* the box   YES   NO   Round about (p. 96)

Identifies at least seven pictures of common objects   YES   NO

Points to five parts of doll on request, (hair, eyes, nose, mouth, legs etc.)   YES   NO   What's it called (p. 81)

Listens to stories   YES   NO

Points to familiar person or toys on request   YES   NO   What shall we do now (p. 123)

Anticipates body movements when nursery rhymes are said   YES   NO

Shows by behaviour he understands several words   YES   NO   What's that noise (p. 51)

Responds to words, e.g. 'where's daddy' – looks around etc.   YES   NO

(*continued on next page*)

Chart 3: Understanding Language *continued*

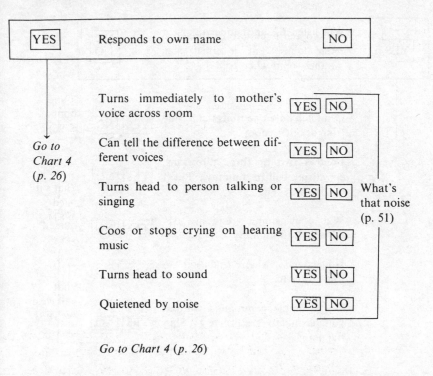

Go to Chart 4 (*p. 26*)

Chart 4: Following Commands

Booklets

YES	Will go and fetch two or three different objects at a time from another room when told	NO

Go to
Chart 5
(p. 27)

Can fetch only one object at a time from another room   YES NO

Follows two or three directions, e.g. 'Bring ball to mummy', 'Put it on the table' etc.   YES NO

Will obey simple requests, e.g. 'Give ball to mummy'.   YES NO

Telling
yourself
(p. 165)

Understands when told *not* to touch toy etc.   YES NO

Obeys simple commands without you having to gesture, e.g. 'Shut the door'   YES NO

Comprehends simple commands if you use gestures, e.g. 'Wave bye-bye'   YES NO

Getting the
message
across
(p. 71)

Responds to No   YES NO

Go to Chart 5 (p. 27)

Chart 5: Imitation of Sounds

Booklets

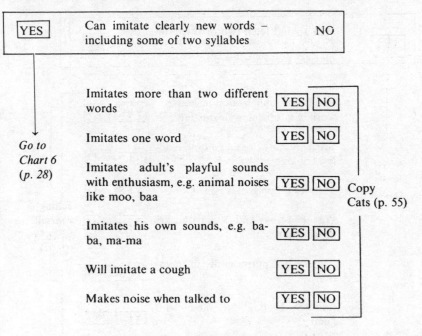

	Can imitate clearly new words – including some of two syllables	
YES		NO

Go to Chart 6 (p. 28)

Imitates more than two different words   YES NO

Imitates one word   YES NO

Imitates adult's playful sounds with enthusiasm, e.g. animal noises like moo, baa   YES NO   Copy Cats (p. 55)

Imitates his own sounds, e.g. ba-ba, ma-ma   YES NO

Will imitate a cough   YES NO

Makes noise when talked to   YES NO

Go to Chart 6 (p. 28)

Chart 6: Imitative Play

Booklets

| YES | Imitates correctly a *sequence* of actions in housework, e.g. brushes up dust into pan and empties it | NO |

Go to Chart 7 (p. 29)

Imitates a single action in house-work, e.g. brushing or dusting   YES NO

Briefly imitates kissing a doll, read-ing book etc.   YES NO

Imitates tapping of a pencil   YES NO

Waves bye-bye and does patacake in imitation   YES NO

Rings a bell purposefully in imita-tion   YES NO

Imitates beating on table with hand   YES NO

Imitates sticking tongue out   YES NO

Copy Cats (p. 55)

Go to Chart 7 (p. 29)

Chart 7: Make-believe Play

Booklets

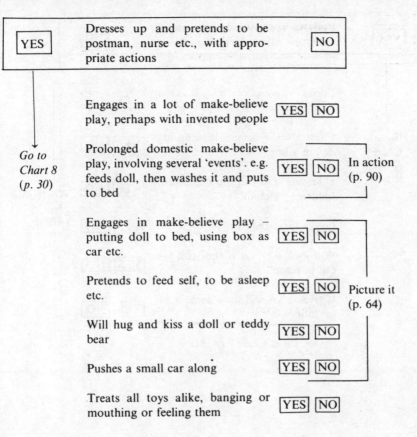

YES | Dresses up and pretends to be postman, nurse etc., with appropriate actions | NO

Go to Chart 8 (p. 30)

Engages in a lot of make-believe play, perhaps with invented people | YES NO

Prolonged domestic make-believe play, involving several 'events'. e.g. feeds doll, then washes it and puts to bed | YES NO | In action (p. 90)

Engages in make-believe play – putting doll to bed, using box as car etc. | YES NO

Pretends to feed self, to be asleep etc. | YES NO | Picture it (p. 64)

Will hug and kiss a doll or teddy bear | YES NO

Pushes a small car along | YES NO

Treats all toys alike, banging or mouthing or feeling them | YES NO

Go to Chart 8 (p. 30)

Chart 8: Objects

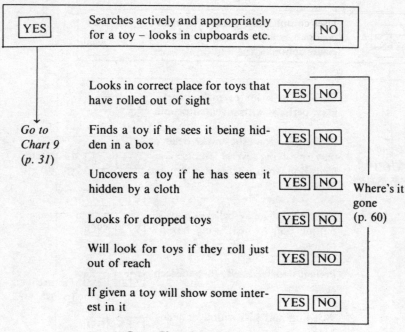

| YES | Searches actively and appropriately for a toy – looks in cupboards etc. | NO |

Go to
Chart 9
(p. 31)

Looks in correct place for toys that have rolled out of sight	YES NO
Finds a toy if he sees it being hidden in a box	YES NO
Uncovers a toy if he has seen it hidden by a cloth	YES NO
Looks for dropped toys	YES NO
Will look for toys if they roll just out of reach	YES NO
If given a toy will show some interest in it	YES NO

Where's it
gone
(p. 60)

Go to Chart 9 (p. 31)

Chart 9: Gestures

Booklets

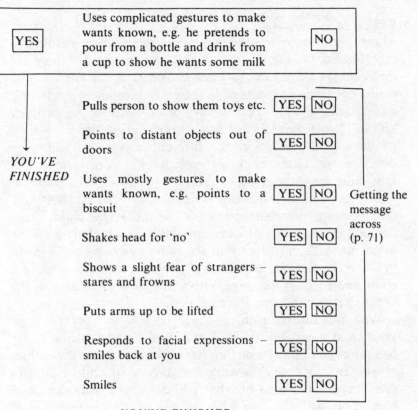

YES | Uses complicated gestures to make wants known, e.g. he pretends to pour from a bottle and drink from a cup to show he wants some milk | NO

YOU'VE FINISHED

Pulls person to show them toys etc. | YES | NO

Points to distant objects out of doors | YES | NO

Uses mostly gestures to make wants known, e.g. points to a biscuit | YES | NO

Shakes head for 'no' | YES | NO

Getting the message across (p. 71)

Shows a slight fear of strangers – stares and frowns | YES | NO

Puts arms up to be lifted | YES | NO

Responds to facial expressions – smiles back at you | YES | NO

Smiles | YES | NO

YOU'VE FINISHED

We shall now discuss the ways in which you could find the charts helpful.

Language development

There is a lot more to language development than learning to talk. Indeed, talking is just the tip of the iceberg, for there are many things a child has to learn before he starts talking. The charts cover nine aspects of language development, including understanding what people say, being able to copy others and to play imaginatively. At this point all we want to do is to draw your attention to different aspects of language development. Later on in the book, we will show how important these are in learning to talk.

But as well as showing what is involved in language development, the charts also outline the stages children go through in each area of development. In each chart we have listed the skills in order, with the more advanced skills given first and the earliest, last. Thus if you start at the bottom of a chart and read *up* the page, you will follow the stages in the order that the children develop them.

With this information, you will be able to find the stage your child has reached. You may find that he is not as far behind as you thought or that he is poorer in some areas than others. In any case, knowing the stage your child is at will give you a better idea of what you can reasonably expect of him. You will then be able to decide which games and activities are suitable for him.

Observing your child's language

However, you can only find out the stage of development your child has reached by observing what he can do. And before you can observe properly you need to know what to look for. This is where the charts can help. For example, take the item in Chart 1, 'Uses twenty clear words'. A very useful exercise (especially if your child is just starting to talk) is to keep a list of the words he uses; but note the word 'clear'. It's there because the words should be understood by everyone,

not just the parents or family. You can check with neighbours or teachers whether they understand them.

How often?
Some of the items ask how often the child does a particular
thing, e.g. 'Babbles constantly' or 'Puts two words together'.
In order to observe what your child does, you should set
aside a certain time when you are free from other distractions, just to observe your child. Choose a time when he is
particularly talkative, and maybe have another child playing
with him or even another adult (dad can observe while mum
plays – then swop over). On a sheet of paper, write down the
items you want to observe, but choose only a few at a time.

Make a stroke against the item every time your child does
it. Here is an example:

Uses nouns	///// ///// ///// ///// ///
Uses action words	///// //

Uses one word at a time	///// ///// ///// ///// ///
Uses two words together	//

Length of time observing – ten minutes

From this, you can see that the child is speaking mostly in
single words and rarely uses two-word utterances. Also, he
uses many more nouns than verbs. If you repeat this exercise
fairly regularly (e.g. every month), you will be able to chart
changes in the child's language.

You can also use this sort of scheme, if your child is at the
babbling stage, to find out where he babbles most. With some
children this will be in the bathroom because the noise is
amplified. Count how often he babbles in a variety of rooms
over the same length of time.

No doubt you will be able to think of many other situations where you can use this scheme.

Testing your child
For some other items, you will need to get the child to do
things for you. This is particularly so in the 'Understanding

Language' and the 'Imitation' charts. This requires some skill on your part, for you have to be sure that your child is co-operating. It is often better to tackle these items indirectly, e.g. within play activities, where you can start off with things you know he can do before introducing the 'new' ones as a variation of the game. Of course, you have to give the child more than one attempt at each thing; indeed the more the better, but keep a careful check on the number of times he does or does not, do the item (see previous example). If he only does it once or twice but tries it ten or more times, then you cannot say that he has passed that item.

Recording your child's language skills

The charts are also designed to form a record of your child's language development.

In order to do this, you should tick the items either YES or NO, depending on whether the child can do them or not.

1. If you tick YES to the first item in the charts (the boxed item) there is no need to answer the remaining items within that chart as they will probably no longer apply to your child. Go on to the next chart.

2. If you tick NO to the boxed item, we suggest you answer *all* the items within that chart.
   Tick YES if the child *can* do that item, even though he may have grown out of it and now rarely does it, e.g. if the child is now putting three words together regularly then tick YES to the item, 'Puts two words together'.
   Tick NO if the child *cannot* do it.

3. Many of the questions you will be able to answer straight away. For others, you will have to observe your child to see just what he can do (see p. 32). Remember you need to have seen the child show the skill on a number of different occasions before you can tick YES.

4. In order to record your child's progress, you could complete the charts using different coloured ink on each occasion. Note the date at which you used each colour.

Guide to booklets

In Part 2 of the Introduction (p. 18) we outlined the sections you would find suitable for your child. However, as each section contains a number of different booklets, each dealing with a specific topic, some of them might be more appropriate than others. This is where the charts could be useful. You will have noticed that beside some of the items in the charts we have given the names of certain booklets. If you have ticked NO to the item, or one of the items covered by the brackets for that booklet, then we suggest you look at that booklet. However, if there are any other items further down the charts which you have ticked NO, then see those booklets first.

By now, we hope you know the sections and/or booklets you should concentrate on. But before you start the games and activities have a look at the next page, 'Points to Remember'.

PART 4: POINTS TO REMEMBER

Now we want to suggest some ways in which you can make the games become more effective in helping your child's language. One thing we should stress is that you must not be too discouraged if you feel you are getting nowhere. Language takes a long time to learn and there are no short cuts. You need to persevere even though there seems to be little or no progress. This is probably the secret of success, for most 'failures' to improve the child's language result from giving up too soon.

However, if the games are to be effective, then there are some points you must always bear in mind.

1. *Make it enjoyable for the child* – Find out what the child particularly likes and use this during the game as a reward when he does what you want him to do. This could be things to eat (like sweets, ice-cream, apples, pieces of cheese) or things to drink; but even a rough and tumble game, looking at a book, playing a particular game or having a record played, can all be used to encourage the child and make the game enjoyable.

You must avoid the danger of making the game into an exercise or letting it become a chore either for you or the child. This often hinders rather than helps the child's learning, and can be very wearing on your patience.

2. *Keep control* – If you are going to help your child to learn new things then it is important that you should be in control and that the child does not do only what he wants to do. Often you can regain this control by ignoring him when he's unco-operative or misbehaves. Do *not* coax him. If you do, you are admitting that he is in control. The best thing to do is to say nothing; just carry on with the game as you want it

played. If he continues to mess around or misuses the play material, then take it away from him and walk out of the room. Wait for a minute or two, then try again. If he continues to misbehave, leave it to another day. However, it's surprising how quickly children will come round to your way of doing it if you make it clear that you are in charge.

3. *Watch your language* – Unintentionally we often make it difficult for the child to learn language because of the way we ourselves use it. Beware of:

talking too much, so that your child doesn't get a chance to say anything;

asking too many questions, so that you are only squeezing language out of the child – he doesn't learn anything from being asked, 'what's that?';

using complicated language, using a dozen words when trying to teach the child one;

talking and not doing – if the child is to learn the meaning of words, then he has to see them 'in action'. You have to make clear to him what it is you are talking about. In short, actions really do speak louder than words for children.

4. *Do it regularly* – Rather than squeezing the games into a spare moment, set aside a certain amount of time *each* day when you can concentrate on playing with your child. The length of time will vary from child to child, but you could start off with a small amount of time (two to three minutes) and then gradually increase it.

5. *Be an opportunist* – Pick a time when you are most likely to get your child's co-operation: a time when he is alert and responsive. Make use of any opportunities that arise during the day to join in with your child's play and to further his language.

6. *Be specific* – Concentrate on one thing at a time and give your child plenty of practice at it before introducing new topics. Know in detail what you are aiming for, e.g. in babbling games you should concentrate on one particular sound at a time.

7.   *Take small steps* – Start off each time with something the child can do before going on to a new topic. But only make *small* changes at a time – move forward in small steps rather than big jumps!

8.   *Don't give up too soon* – Children need to get used to a game, so keep at it, even though you seem to be getting nowhere. But even if your child has mastered a game, continue to give him practice at it.

9.   *Record progress* – It is very easy to overlook, and indeed forget about, the progress which your child makes. To avoid this, keep a record of your child's language. In Part 3 of the Introduction we mentioned ways in which you can do this (see p. 33). These records will be a source of encouragement for you as you read back over them.

Finally, as you play with your child, think about whether another game, or variation of the one you are using, might be better for him. The games we suggest are guidelines for all parents, but often the best games are those specially designed for individual children. Always think how you could adapt the games to suit your child.

We hope you and your child enjoy the games – have fun!

SECTION 1: THE FOUNDATIONS OF LANGUAGE

Booklet 1: Babbling on
Booklet 2: What's that noise?
Booklet 3: Copy cats
Booklet 4: Where's it gone?
Booklet 5: Picture it
Booklet 6: Getting the message across

INTRODUCTION

The booklets in this section are designed primarily to help children who have not yet started to talk. They are concerned with the foundations of language development and describe ways of fostering the skills a child should have in order to learn language. However, as some of these skills are important throughout all language development, we will be referring to them in other sections of the book.

The first booklet describes how to encourage the child to *make sounds* and to exercise his speech organs.

The second booklet is concerned with *listening*, particularly in helping your child to recognise different sounds; to locate them and to attend to your voice without being distracted by other noises.

The third booklet is on *imitation*. A child must be able to copy an adult model in order to learn his mother tongue, and children have to acquire the ability to do this.

Until a child can recognise people and objects, he cannot be expected to name them. The fourth booklet shows how such *recognition* can be helped.

The fifth booklet is concerned with *pretending* or *make-believe*. Only when a child begins to play imaginary games can we be sure that he has the ability to make mental images. This is essential to language development.

The last booklet in this section (number six) is about *communication*. Even before a child says his first word you can help him to communicate his wants and to understand you. This booklet should prove especially useful to parents of children whose speech is very delayed.

BOOKLET 1: BABBLING ON

When a child first sits at a piano and presses down the keys for his own amusement, the noise does not sound much like a Beethoven sonata. Similarly with the child's early vocalisations; his coos and gurgles and grunts do not sound much like speech. But both serve the same purpose – that of gaining control and co-ordination of an instrument, while at the same time finding out how to produce certain sounds.

Some handicapped children are rather flabby and sluggish and do not practice kicking and moving their arms and legs as much as other children. They have to be encouraged to do this. In the same way, some children are too quiet and do not play at making sounds. With these children it is especially important actively to encourage sound play.

Encouraging sound play
Before you start on this, spend a little time observing where your child is most 'talkative'.

In the bathroom – some children vocalise more in one room than in another, so it is well worth while doing some experimenting. See if your child makes more sounds in the bathroom than in other rooms. People often like to sing in the bathroom because their voice is amplified and sounds good, and children may become more 'talkative' there for the same reason. Do all you can to encourage this enjoyment; sing and talk and laugh with your child. Be active and animated; avoid a monotonous tone of voice or gloomy expressions.

The bathroom mirror is also useful. Sit your child in front of it, so that he can see his mouth moving while he makes sounds. You may have to sit behind him at first and make sounds to your own reflection, in order to get him started. Alternatively, you may have to tickle him or jog him up and down. With any luck, he will get to the point of practising by himself.

Using little toys – children's early sound play often goes with active enjoyment · or excitement. Sometimes certain toys will encourage a child to vocalise. You might experiment by hanging small toys on elastic, so that they bob up and down when he touches them; we often find this starts a child vocalising. Once he has begun to do this, be sure to enter into the enjoyment. Answer his sounds, laugh and play with him.

Another way of increasing vocalisation is with a little toy held in the hand. Every time your child makes a sound, waggle the toy or make it jump up into the air immediately. When he is silent, keep it still. If you keep this up, he will soon get the idea that whenever he makes a sound, things start to happen.

Switch on

If none of these games work with your child, here is another idea. Set aside about ten minutes every day when you will not be interrupted. At this time, bring in a torch or reading lamp which your child does not normally see. Each time your child makes a sound, switch the light on for a couple of seconds, then switch it off until he makes another sound. (It is important that the child can see the light but place it out of his reach.) You may find that he gets the idea very quickly and every time you bring the lamp in, he will start 'talking'. After a time, you may not wish to encourage every sound; perhaps you will switch the light on only when he makes a loud sound.

If your child is partially sighted he still might enjoy this game, if you use a bright light. Or alternatively, you could sound a bell or buzzer every time he 'talks', rather than flash the light.

Clown

A handyman may be able to make a 'clown' whose 'eyes' will light up and who bleeps at the press of a switch (see Figure 1). You can use this in the same way as the light, but it will

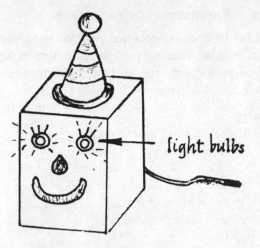

Flashing clown

Fig. 1

light bulbs

hole

Hole in the wall

Fig. 2

probably be even more enjoyable for the child. Alternatively, you might be able to find such a toy in the shops – but remember, don't let the child play with it when you are not there. Keep it for use in this game only.

Babbling

We said that a child's first sound play is rather like his first experience of banging the key on a piano. His babble, though, is more like an instrument tuning up for a concert. Little snatches are played over and over again.

This is just what a child does when he starts babbling. Now he will repeat sounds in strings, e.g. ma-ma-ma, ga-ga-ga, la-la-la and so on.

At this stage, he may learn to imitate new sounds if you start keeping up a dialogue with him. When he says 'baba', then you answer him, either by copying his 'baba' or by saying 'baby'. Keep this rhythmic and lively and do not answer him in an automatic way, or this will be discouraging. Let him watch your change of expression as well.

Many of the games described earlier can also be used at this stage. You can also introduce some variations. For example, switch the light on only when your child vocalises after you. When he begins to do this regularly, switch the light on only when his vocalisations sound like yours. If he can say 'gigi', then you say 'give me' and switch the light on for a good copy.

But in all these games, let your voice go up and down, loud and soft. Listening is just as important as speaking, so make your voice worth listening to!

Hole in the wall

A screen or a large piece of card with a small hole in it, a few inches wide, will often intrigue children and you can use this to encourage their babbling and imitation (see Fig. 2).

You will probably find that your child will push things through the hole without much encouragement. For this game, you place yourself on one side of the screen, with the child on the other. After he pushes a toy through the hole, you push it back. Do this with only one toy until he gets the idea of the game. Then start waiting until he 'talks' before you return the toy. Even tease him in a playful way by letting him see the toy and as soon as he says anything, pop it through the hole to him. After this stage, start returning the toy only when he attempts to copy you, e.g. you say 'ball' and he answers 'ba' and back comes the ball. When he can do this without any trouble, you might even become more strict and return the toy only when his reply sounds just like yours.

A word of warning: although it doesn't take long to read about the stages in this game, you must not be tempted to rush through them. Give your child plenty of practice at each one.

Exercising the tongue and lips

In order to be able to speak we must be able to control the movements of our lips, jaws and tongue. Some children (especially Down's Syndrome) may have large and sluggish tongues which they have to learn to keep inside their mouths. If your child is inclined to let his tongue hang out, you might threaten to catch it every time you see it. He should soon learn to stick it in before you can do so.

You also need to encourage him to 'exercise' his tongue. For example, you could put a tiny sweet on the tip of his tongue. He will then have to draw his tongue in carefully to get the sweet into his mouth. Licking lollipops or ice-cream will also help to keep his tongue flexible. Try holding the lollipop to the right and to the left, so that he must move his tongue around to lick it. A drop of honey on the upper lip, chin or cheek will also get his tongue moving, as he tries to lick it off.

Chewing

However, the games with lollipops or honey should not be over done. The sugar in them is not only bad for the child's teeth; it is also bad for his general health, especially as many handicapped children will become overweight unless they are kept on a sensible diet.

Much more important in speech development is the exercise which comes from chewing with the mouth shut. Some handicapped children do have difficulty with chewing, but it is not wise to keep them on sloppy food. You may have to introduce solid food very gradually, for instance, by adding finely chopped biscuit to his cereal then coarser and coarser pieces until eventually he can chew whole biscuits, meat, carrots, apples etc. This exercise will itself help his speech mechanisms, for in talking just as in chewing we have to move our jaws, lips and tongues. Indeed, chasing food from between our teeth or gums with our tongues is excellent practice for the fine tongue movements required in speech.

Blowing and sucking
This will help your child to experience lip and palate movements. He will enjoy blowing through a straw into some soapy water to make bubbles. Later on, he can blow bubbles into the air.

It is also useful to give him a straw to drink through. Unfortunately, ordinary drinking straws are rather thin and flimsy, so try to get the more sturdy plastic ones or improvise with some other form of tubing.

Most children like to blow out candles or matches, but make sure that they blow with their lips together.

You can play a game with a light feather or a ping-pong ball. Blow it across the table to him, making a 'f' sound as you do it (f-f-f-f-f). Then let him blow it back to you. You can then use straws to blow through – the makings of blow football!

More fun with sounds
When you are a beginner it is often easier to make animal noises than human ones. It will help your child if you let your hair down sometimes and pretend to be a dog or cat or cow etc. Later, you can show him some toy animals or pictures of animals, while making the appropriate animal noise. Get him

to join in making the noises. In this way he is practising sounds he will need when he begins to speak, sounds such as 'm' (moo) and 'b' (baa).

Pop!

Many children like the popping of corks from bottles. As you do this, make an explosive 'pop', pursing your lips as you say it.

Train game

Make a 'train' out of boxes (e.g. matchboxes) and as you push it around the floor, make appropriate train noises (ch-ch-ch). Encourage your child to do the same when he is pushing the train.

Snake game

Here is a game to play with a 's' sound or hissing (s-s-s-s-s). First cut out a circle of paper as in Figure 3 to make a snake. Then lift the snake by the head and as it falls down, make the hissing sound. Encourage your child to imitate, and make the snake fall when he attempts to copy you. Don't worry if your child doesn't do this very well; this is one of the later sounds to be pronounced correctly.

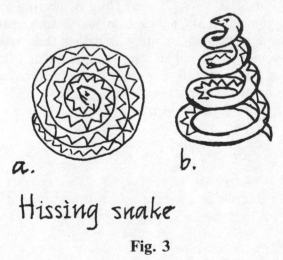

a.   b.

Hissing snake

Fig. 3

Intonation

If we are to be understood by other people we have to learn to use the same intonation as they do. It is often difficult to understand foreigners, not because they are not making the right sounds but because their intonation is strange. That is, their voices are going up and down in the wrong places. Intonation is like a tune – men with deep voices and boys with high-pitched voices can all sing the same tune which can be recognised by others. As a child grows, he usually starts practising these speech rhythms; children often pretend they are reading a book or talking to someone and it really sounds as if they are, but if we listen carefully, we will not be able to recognise a single word. This we call 'jargon'.

We should start encouraging this once the child's babble is well established. One way to do it is to exaggerate the rhythmic part of what we say. You know how children will call out to one another in play 'Com-ing!' making the word a real song. It would help if we did this more than usual to help our child get the idea, until we are almost singing the words 'Tea-time', 'Sit-down', 'Come and Get it!'. We should reward or praise the child for copying these patterns.

Another way in which children are helped at this stage is through nursery rhymes. If your child is showing no interest in these you might try telling him just a small part of the rhyme at a time, and chanting it rather than repeating it monotonously. You might also experiment in using funny voices for the rhyme. If your child finds this hilarious, all to the good for that means he is listening to the speech rhythms, and may try to experiment on his own.

BOOKLET 2: WHAT'S THAT NOISE?

As well as learning to speak, children have to learn to listen. They need to be able to locate sounds in order to know who is speaking. They also have to learn to recognise many different sounds; to know their mother's voice or to recognise father's footsteps for instance. Furthermore, we live in a very noisy world and have to learn to attend to someone talking and to ignore all the other noises in the room. Here are some games to play which will help your child to listen.

First, or course, you must make sure he has no hearing loss. Even a slight hearing loss can make it difficult for him to learn to speak. Also some children, especially those with Down's Syndrome, may have a fluctuating hearing loss brought on by catarrh. They may hear normally one week but not the next. Alternatively, they may hear quite well when you are standing close to them or in front of them but not when you are further away or behind. If you are in any doubt about your child's hearing, it is important to seek advice as early as possible. Your local Health Clinic can arrange for hearing tests.

Experiencing sounds

From an early age a child needs to have plenty of experience with toys which make different sounds. This is just as important as having toys of different shapes and sizes, yet toy manufacturers often seem to overlook this. Toys such as rattles, bells, musical boxes, squeaking toys, push and pull toys which make a noise when moved, cymbals, 'mooing' toys (such as those made by Galts) will be useful, although you can always make your own by filling containers with different substances: such as peas for a loud rattle, or rice for a gentle swish.

Where's that noise?

For this game, you will need a collection of toys which make different sounds, e.g. rattle, squeaky toy, whistle etc. Play the game by squeaking a toy behind the child's back when he is not expecting it, and see if he will turn to the sound. Vary this by squeaking the toy from different parts of the room when the child is not looking, or hide a loudly ticking clock behind a curtain or chair and see whether he can find it.

Later you can make this game still harder, by setting out a series of three cardboard boxes and hiding the clock in one, to see if the child can find it.

What's that noise?

It is a good idea to hang rattles and bells on a string so that he can experiment with them. In this way he will learn to recognise different sounds and know which toy makes a particular sound. Tins can be used for drumming on, and squeezy bottles filled with peas make good maracas.

More sound recognition

When a child goes for a walk, we usually point out things to look at. We should also stop and let him experience the rustling of leaves, snapping of twigs, the whistling of the wind, dogs barking and birdsong, if possible.

A surprise element also helps to get children listening. We can often get their attention by varying the pitch of our own voices, sometimes whispering, sometimes speaking loudly or suddenly.

Music games

Music is important too and there are some attractive musical boxes on the market which may prove useful.

Many more games can be invented if you can play a musical instrument. Remember, you do not need to be a concert performer! For if you can play a few notes on a recorder or mouth organ or glockenspiel, it will do. If you vary what you play and let your child march, skip, pretend to be a giant etc., as the music changes, he will be encouraged to listen, in order to know what to do.

Alternatively, you can use percussion instruments and alter the rhythm – play a marching rhythm on a drum for him to march or a skipping rhythm for him to skip; a monotonous drumming might indicate that it is raining and he must take cover. As well as this you can use records and invent different activities to go with them.

Nursery rhymes
Even before children can understand the *words* of nursery rhymes and action rhymes, they can begin to listen for certain *sounds* to indicate an action, e.g. 'they all fall *down*'.

Fetching games
If you can, tape-record the sounds made by favourite toys and familiar objects, e.g. sound of the drum, a bell, a squeaky toy, a toy dog etc. Place the objects in front of the child and when he hears the sound, he has to pick out the right object. Later the game could be made harder by hiding the object around the room.

Harder games
Once a child has learnt to locate sounds and has begun to associate certain sounds with certain objects or events, you can initiate more difficult games involving pictures.

Hunt the Animal
Cut out or draw some pictures of common animals and mount them on cards (see Figure 4).

Make the appropriate animal noises – meow, woof-woof, moo, baa and quack-quack, in any order – and see whether your child can find the right picture.

Games like these can be graded so that they start very easy and become more difficult. You could start with only the duck picture and show your child what to do when you 'quack' for instance. Later he may get to the point that you

Hunt the animal

Fig. 4

can scatter the pictures around the room and he will search and find the right picture.

This game can be varied with pictures of clocks, drums, spoons etc. instead of animals.

BOOKLET 3: COPY CATS

Imitation

Children often call each other 'copy cats' but we do not always realise the importance of this ability to copy or imitate what others do. Much of what we learn during life is learnt by someone showing us how to do it, so that we can imitate their actions. Certainly, we would never have learnt to talk without this ability. Yet we are not born able to imitate, and some mentally handicapped children find it difficult and need a great deal of help.

Imitation a step at a time

1. At first a child cannot copy other people but only 'copy' himself. He will bang a rattle by chance and then have another go. At this stage one can encourage him by having interesting things for him to swipe at – things which move, or change colour or make a sound. This will encourage him to 'have a go'.
2. The next step is helped if *we* imitate him. He may bang a drum – then *we* do it directly afterwards and then he will do it again. In this way he will go on to the next stage.
3. Now we can *start* an action which we already know he can do. We start off banging the drum when he is not doing this and he will copy us. Until he can do this, he is not ready to imitate anything new.
4. Now we can get him to imitate a new action. Waving bye-bye is one that children often learn to imitate early.
5. When he can imitate several actions like this, we can start to get him to look at our face and imitate us by opening and shutting his mouth, smacking or pursing his lips etc.

We must, of course, make a fuss of him when he starts to imitate actions in the region of his mouth. At first, don't worry about getting him to copy sounds, although you could later help him to produce a sound by patting his mouth with your hand.

6. Now we can start to get him to imitate some sounds. Again, we may have to start by imitating *him* before we can introduce new sounds. We have already made some suggestions in 'Babbling On'. One sound which he may imitate early is a cough. This is a good beginning but, of course, we must not simply leave it at that but try to shape more useful imitations.

If you find that your child can imitate gesture quite well and yet is not imitating sounds, it is as well to make sure that he has no hearing loss (see 'What's that noise?' p. 51).

Does he find it hard to imitate?

We have already suggested that children learn how to imitate and that this ability to imitate greatly helps their development. There are a few children who do not seem to 'get the idea' even when we take imitation a step at a time as suggested above. It will take a lot of patience to get these children to imitate but will be well worth the effort. This is best done with the help of another adult. After giving the child a 'model' of clapping hands, for instance, someone may have to hold his hands and clap them for him. He should then be given a reward immediately. At first the child may not co-operate – he should be rewarded and made a fuss of at the first sign of co-operation (i.e. when he himself does not fight the adult but moves his hands in time with theirs). Gradually, you will find that the second adult has to do less and less, perhaps only touch the child's hands instead of holding his arms and he will 'copy' clapping. For the next action, fewer prompts may be required. Even when encouraging mouth movements, it may be necessary to open his mouth for him or shape his lips etc. before he will be able to copy on his own.

Follow my leader
We can get many ideas from watching children at play and reading about traditional games. Many games are concerned with copying or imitation. *Follow my leader* is one such game. The leader lines the other children up behind him and they have to follow him and 'do what he does': if he bends down, so must they, etc.

O'Grady says
This is another imitating game. It has many versions but the simplest is for the mother, leader or teacher to stand in front of the child and say 'Do this' and the child has to copy the action. The actions should be very simple at first – holding one's hands above one's head or bending down etc. Later make it more complicated by using only one hand, one leg, etc. at a time. This can later be extended into a game with sounds, when the leader makes a noise and the children have to copy it, e.g. baa, moo, woof-woof. At a later stage, these can then be combined with an action which symbolises the animal, e.g. clapping hands in front of face to represent a duck, while saying 'quack-quack'.

Having something to copy
It is important to play with your child and to give him something worthwhile to copy or imitate. Unless he sees you doing things he is unlikely to do them. For example, show him how he can play with some of his toys; pushing toy cars along while making engine noises, cradling and rocking a doll or teddy etc.

At first you may have to take his hands and 'make' him do the actions, e.g. hold his hand on the toy car while you push it along. Also it is good to have two similar toys, so that he can do what you are doing at the same time, rather than waiting until you have finished and he can have the toy.

Housework
Also, give him a chance to imitate the things you do around the house (mopping, dusting etc.) by being allowed to watch

and having a duster or broom of his own. When he sees you do something, let him have a try, e.g. taking screw tops off bottles or laying the table.

Mirrors

Children can learn a lot by watching themselves in a mirror, and in particular they can see their own mouth movements. Ideally, the mirror should be fairly large, preferably attached to the wall at ground level so that the child can sit or lie comfortably in front of it.

Copying sounds

Here is a game that is particularly useful to get your child copying sounds. Choose something that your child particularly likes, e.g. ice-cream, jelly, lemonade (something that doesn't need much chewing). This is what you do:

1. Sit yourself and your child opposite to one another at the table. To establish a ritual, give your child a small portion when he looks at your face. When he does this reward him *immediately*.

2. 'Model' your child's sounds – that is, you say 'baba' or 'mama' or 'dada' or whatever sounds he is already able to make and only reward the child when he both looks at you and makes a sound. At first, this need not be very like the sound you made; reward him for any sound he makes in reply. Do not reward crying or bad behaviour – just ignore this.

3. When the child is regularly making a sound in reply to your model, then only reward him when he imitates the sounds you made – NOT when he makes a different sound in answer to yours.

4. Now you can 'model' a sound which, although like the sounds your child is already making, is not quite the same, for instance, 'bye-bye' instead of 'ba-ba' or 'ta-ta' instead of 'da-da.

5. Reward fair approximations to these new sounds at first but when your child starts to imitate the new sounds then reward only *good* approximations.

6. Continue in this way until your child can imitate new sounds well.

7. Soon you will be able to introduce *words* which can be formed naturally from the sounds he is making already, i.e. 'ball' instead of 'ba'. When you model 'ball', let the child see a real ball or a picture of a ball as well as hearing the word. It will take quite a long time to achieve this, and it will require all your artistry and knowledge of the child to do it well. But most important it will need plenty of practice. Incidentally, you can equally well play this game with other types of 'reward', e.g. making a light come on, or handing him a particular toy (see the Booklet, 'Babbling On' p. 44).

BOOKLET 4: WHERE'S IT GONE?

Before a child can speak for himself he has to understand. This does not simply mean understanding what other people say: children also have to understand the world around them. They are not born with the ability to make sense of what they see; it is something they have to learn to do. *We* know that an object is a cup even when it is handed to us upside-down, but a baby does not. He may even be frightened by a familiar object which he does not recognise because he is seeing it from an unfamiliar angle. A baby can be frightened by the sight of his own mother if she is wearing a different hat!

Some older mentally handicapped children are still at this stage of uncertainty. They will need help in recognising familiar objects; for until they can do this with some degree of certainty they will not be ready to start naming them.

Furthermore, young children think that objects no longer exist if they cannot see them. This is why a young child will not search for a sweet under a carton even though he has seen you hide it there.

When the child first starts to search for things, it is a sign that he is beginning to understand the nature of objects. As this understanding develops, he will search more intelligently, for instance go straight to the place where the object was last seen.

The games in this booklet will help the child to recognise objects and to search for them when they are hidden.

Peek-a-boo

This game is not only enjoyed by nearly all children, but it helps them realise that objects still exist even though they can't see them. You can play it by covering your face with a cloth and slowly pulling it off, or you can hide behind a chair, curtain or door and jump out. You can also make a toy disappear behind your back, into a bag or box, and make · it re-appear.

Hiding Games

1. Hide a sweet or a tiny favourite toy under a carton. Let your child see you do this but do not let him touch until you are ready. Show him your empty hand and encourage him to find the sweet.

2. Have two empty cartons (or plastic flower-pots or tins) instead of one and pretend to hide the sweet under the first carton but really keep it in your hand and hide it under the second one.

   As before, show the child your empty hand and encourage him to find the sweet. Watch where he looks first.

   When he can find the sweet from under one of two empty cartons, try making the game more difficult by introducing another carton.

3. Place an empty carton on a tray but have a screen between you and the child so that he cannot see you hiding the sweet under the carton. Let him see the sweet before you begin and show him your empty hand when you have finished. Then remove the screen and encourage him to search for the sweet. You can make this game more difficult by gradually introducing more cartons and not always hiding the sweet in the same place.

   In all these games make a big fuss of him when he is successful.

Special Place

It is also worth keeping some of the child's toys in a special place, for example, his favourite ball in the same corner of a cupboard. Not only will this make it easier for him to find it but it will help him realise that objects don't disappear when they are out of sight.

Where shall I look?

Another important aspect of learning about the world is knowing what happens to objects under various circumstances, for example, if you see a toy train going into a tunnel you know from experience in which direction it's travelling, and where to look for it coming out. This is part of understanding the world. You can help a child reach this understanding by playing some of the following games:

Make a tunnel by cutting a large cardboard tube in half. Tie strings to matchbox cars and thread the string through the tunnel. Then pull the car slowly through the tunnel so that the child sees it disappear. At first he may expect it to come out the way it went in – later he may move to the other end of the tunnel to watch the car emerge (see Figure 5). (Note: You may have to anchor your tunnel to a base to prevent your child from picking it up and looking underneath and so spoiling the game.) You can buy or make other toys, such as marble runs, which will help your child to get an idea of direction. At a simpler level, you can hide his Teddy behind your back and make it pop out the other side. Note where he begins to look for it.

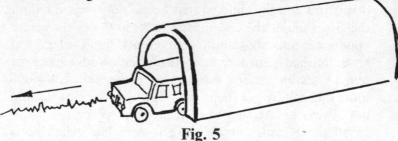

Fig. 5

Why did that happen?

Children also have to learn about cause and effect. They are not born knowing that if you drop something out of the pram it falls to the ground, or that if you press a switch a light will come on.

If he has a toy with a long string attached, he will not at first realise that he can reach the toy by pulling the string.

You can help him to learn this by putting the string in his hand and gradually moving the toy further away.

Another toy which will help your child to learn about cause and effect is a wooden doll that you can buy at most toy shops, and which hangs on the wall. When a string is pulled, the arms and legs will move (see Figure 6).

If your child is good with his hands, push/pull moving toys are also helpful (see Figure 7).

Undoubtedly, you will be able to think of many variations of these games that will help your child's understanding of the world.

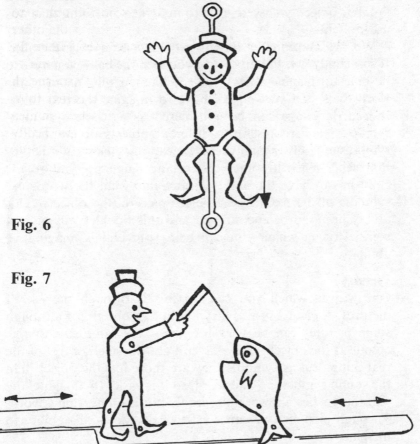

Fig. 6

Fig. 7

BOOKLET 5: PICTURE IT

Before you read any more, close your eyes and picture in your mind a cup of tea (or something stronger if you like!). What you have just done is create a 'mental' picture of a familiar object: you were able to imagine something that was not present.

We are continually having to do this in everyday life. If somebody says to you, 'Have you seen the ball?' you have to be able to imagine what a ball is like. In this instance, the word 'ball' is a *symbol*, we have to imagine the real thing. Indeed, language can be considered as a whole system of symbols, each representing different objects or events. But symbols are only meaningful if we can imagine what it is they represent. When it comes to learning language symbols the child has to have the ability to imagine what the words are symbols of: he has to be able to 'picture' the objects. This ability needs to be encouraged and this booklet will suggest some ways in which you can help your child's imaginative ability.

Pictures

One way in which you can do this is through the use of pictures. A picture is also a symbol of an object, for although some pictures can be very life-like – the same size, shape, colour as the object – they haven't got the smell or feel of the real thing. But as symbols they are more like the object than the sound symbol, i.e. the word, so it is easier to 'imagine' the real thing when shown a picture than it is on hearing a word. Through pictures one can start to help the child's ability to imagine.

General hints

1. The first pictures you should use are ones of objects that the child is very familiar with, e.g. his drinking cup, ball, teddy bear, shoes etc.
2. The pictures should be as life-like as possible – preferably the same size and colour as the real thing.
3. Have only one object on each page, or better still, mount each picture on a piece of card.

This will probably mean that you will have to make your own pictures. You could attempt to draw them or else have photographs taken (preferably coloured but if these are black and white, try colouring them). It is also important that the object really stands out on the page. You can do this by:

(a) making the background a contrasting colour to the object (plain backgrounds are best as they have no distractions).

(b) drawing a black line around the outline of the object so as to emphasise its shape.

However, Learning Development Aids have produced a set of sixteen early pictures on gummed paper (Early Language Stamps) so that they can be stuck into books or on to cards. You might find these are useful at this stage.

Once the child has started to recognise pictures, you can begin using less familiar pictures, e.g. other cups of different sizes, colours etc. Ultimately the child should be able to recognise symbolic drawings which have very little resemblance to the real thing, like those in Figure 8.

Now for some picture games you could play.

Fig. 8

Hiding Game

Collect a number of tins or cardboard boxes big enough to cover some of the child's favourite toys or familiar objects, for instance, his drinking cup. On one of the boxes attach a picture of the cup and always hide the cup under this box. At first, use only this box; hiding the cup under it and encouraging the child to find it (have some of the child's favourite drink in the cup so that he will want to find the cup, and give him a drink when he does). Once he's grasped the idea of the game, you can then start using another box – the same size, colour and shape as the other, except this one has *no* picture. Now the child has to choose between two boxes but the picture will always show where the cup is. The child should learn quickly that the picture means 'here is the cup'. Once he can pick the right box out of two, you can introduce other boxes so that he has to choose from four or five. (Remember to shuffle the boxes after you've hidden the object.) Once the child has learnt to find one object by looking at the picture, you can start the whole game with a different object.

Around the house

You can extend the hiding game by putting the picture of the object in different places around the house. As before, use the picture to show where the object is hidden: for instance, if the child's cup is in a cupboard in the kitchen then stick the picture on the cupboard door. When he wants a drink, encourage him to find the cup. Of course, you should vary the place where the cup is kept so that he really has to look.

Take your pick

Once the child can find several objects in the hiding game, you can make the game harder by having him pick one picture out of a number of pictures. This time have two boxes, *each* with a different picture of an object. (At the beginning it's best to have two very different objects for this game.) Hide *one* object under the appropriate box, change the position of the boxes and, as before, encourage the child to find the object.

Now the child has to look very carefully at the pictures to find which is the right one. If he picks the wrong box, show him where it is and then start again. If he gets it right, make a great fuss and give him a little 'reward' – a sweet, drink of juice etc. Remember to vary the position of the boxes each time.

Fetching game
Scatter a few of the child's favourite toys or familiar objects around the room. The idea is for the child to fetch you one of these when you show him a picture of the object you want. At first, have only one object; show him the picture and take him to the object, lift it and compare it to the picture. Practice this a few times, then let him do it by himself. When he has learnt to bring the one object, put down a few more objects so that he has to pick the toy. Again you may have to go with him and compare each toy with the picture, saying no, shaking your head if it's not the same; but being pleased if it is. Encourage him to do this by himself. Gradually you can make the game more difficult, either by:
1.   Having more objects, and using pictures of all the objects, e.g. if you have ten objects, have ten pictures, show the child one picture at a time, getting him to fetch that object until he has brought you all ten objects;
2.   Introducing pictures that are less life-like (see above, page 65): instead of having a picture of a cup exactly like the child's cup, for example, cut out a picture from a magazine or draw a cup.

Picture-books
You can extend the hiding and fetching games by using the pictures by themselves. These might well be made into the child's first picture-book – but have only one picture per page. As you go through the pictures with the child, pretend to be doing something with the object, for instance, if it's a cup – drink from it; or a ball – pretend to kick it. Encourage the child to copy you and, of course, name the object and get him to do the same. Eventually as you look through the

pictures he should be able to show that he has recognised them by doing an appropriate action or attempting to say the word.

Learning Development Aids are producing some picture-books designed to help children recognise pictures (Barnaby Books – Learn to Look series).

However, you can also get the child interested in pictures at an earlier stage. Here are two examples:

Picture Cube

Paste some pictures of familiar objects on to all the sides of a small cardboard box, or a cube made of polystyrene (see Figure 9). This should be at least 6 × 6 × 6 in. You can then use it in throwing or kicking games, naming the picture the child is looking at every time you hand him the box. Or the child can have fun simply rolling the cube over and making different pictures appear.

Picture cube

Fig. 9

Picture Roundabout

Another way of using the cube is as a 'roundabout'. To do this, stick a large knitting needle through the middle of the cube (see Figure 10). Holding the needle by its sharp end, the child (or you) can then spin the cube, making different pictures appear. Very little effort is required to make the cube move. This makes it particularly useful with physically handicapped children who cannot move around easily, or who find it difficult to hold a book.

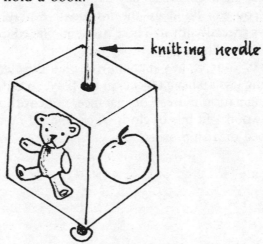

knitting needle

Picture roundabout
Fig. 10

Pretending

Pretending games are another very good way of building up your child's imagination, and thus helping his language development. You can start these pretending games by looking at pictures, or, better still, with toys.

What you should aim to encourage is make-believe play with toys. The earliest form of make-believe play usually centres around a doll or a teddy bear, with the child pretending that it is a person. He may cuddle, pat or kiss it. You can model these actions for your child and encourage him to copy you. Later you can start doing different actions with the dolls: feeding them from toy cups, putting them to bed or washing them. You will often have to demonstrate this sort of play with the child and encourage him to join in. Remember though that it is play; don't make it too much of a lesson, and the more you enter into the spirit of the game, the more likely he is to join in with you.

By the way, boys as well as girls can enjoy and benefit from this sort of doll play, for they are simply reliving with the dolls the events that they experience.

You can build up the imaginative play by keeping some toys specially for it. These are then placed carefully away and not just thrown into a toy box.

As your child's imaginative play develops, you can start using less realistic objects in the play, so that he has to use his imagination more. For instance, use cardboard boxes, pieces of wood, old bits of cloth. A cardboard box could be used as a bed or a ship or a TV!

BOOKLET 6: GETTING THE MESSAGE ACROSS

Language is only one way of communicating with other people, or 'getting the message across'. Babies are already communicating with their mothers before language has developed. They smile or cry or struggle and use gestures to make themselves understood. And these methods of communicating are not lost as we grow older: we still nod and shake our heads, and our facial expressions help to convey our meaning.

For handicapped children, who are often slow to develop spoken language and some of whom will always be poor speakers, these other means of expression are particularly important. We need to encourage alternative means of communication so that the children do not become unduly frustrated, or sink into lethargy; though of course alternative means of expression do not take the place of the spoken word, which always needs to be encouraged, but only supplement it.

By using gestures we can for instance, give a child a means of conveying his choice of food or toys, and of letting us know why he is sad or excited, or that he has a pain.

What is being suggested here is not something new. We do it with babies anyway. For instance, we show them how to wave 'bye-bye', by waving with them and sometimes actually moving their arm. In this way babies learn to use a universally understood gesture before they learn to speak. They can often shake their heads for 'no' and nod for 'yes'.

Use of such consistent gestures can greatly help the handicapped child by giving him ways of making his wants known while his speech is still inarticulate, or before he has learnt to talk.

General Hints

1. Your child needs to *want* to communicate before he will make the effort. You must make some demands of him and not anticipate his every need immediately, e.g. sometimes stop in the middle of a rough and tumble game and say 'Do you want some more?', then wait until he nods before continuing.

2. It is important to give your child some *choice*. Having to choose between alternatives is helping him to think and to become independent.

3. The gestures you use must be consistent. You must always use the *same* gesture for 'sit down' for instance. Not only you, but all the family should agree on what gestures to use.

4. Your child will learn to use these gestures by imitation. You must give him a *clear* model, i.e. you may have to nod your head or beckon in an exaggerated way.

5. When you use a gesture, like beckoning, *always* use words as well, i.e. 'Come here'. If your child is able to speak, encourage both the gesture and the words.

Some early examples:

When your child is playing with his food, as well as saying, 'Eat it up!' use the gesture of taking imaginary food to your mouth and chewing.

When you want your child to come to you, use a beckoning gesture, while saying 'Come here!'. Reward your child with a hug, or even a small sweet, when he comes.

When you say 'sit down!' use both hands in a downward sweep.

In the booklet 'What's it called?' (p. 82) we have described a game to play with your child to help him to understand the names of objects and to bring his favourite toys when you name them. It is worth trying to link your demand also with a gesture, that is, when asking for a 'ball' you use the gesture of throwing something in the air, or you touch your shoe when asking for a 'shoe', and so on.

You are probably already using some gestures in this way but it is important to extend their use and to be absolutely consistent. And although you may use these gestures, does your child? He may need some encouragement, so directly he starts to copy your gesture you should reward him by showing you have understood, and are pleased.

Pointing

A child can usually show you what he wants when it is in reach. He may even not need to show you, he just takes it! However, children often have to be taught how to point to something which is out of reach. How can we teach them this?

As soon as a child can reach out for his favourite toy or sweet, you can begin to teach him to point. You can do this by holding the toy a little further away, so that he is reaching for it, but not touching it. Directly he puts his hand in the direction of the toy, give it to him. Next time increase the distance. When your child is putting his hand out for distant toys, show him the 'pointing' gesture and hold his hand in this position.

Nod for 'Yes'

A child can convey quite a lot if he can nod and shake his head, to indicate 'yes' or 'no' consistently. It is worth the effort to teach him to do this. You may be able to do it just by imitation. Hold up something he likes and say 'Do you want it?' and stand in front of him and nod your head. Immediately he nods, give it to him. Make sure that it *is* what he wants. If he does not get the idea, get another person to help you and stand behind the child and gently rock his head after your 'model'. As before he should get the object as soon as he 'nods'. Do this until he starts nodding without the prompt.

Shake for 'No'

This is more difficult to teach. You will have to choose a time when you are doing something with the child which he does *not* like. As before show him a model of head-shaking, and immediately he copies it stop doing what he doesn't like. Again, you may need someone else to help to 'prompt' the child by moving his head. Once a child has learnt these two gestures, he can communicate a great deal in a way which is much preferable to screams or tantrums, and everyone will be able to understand him.

Games to play
We can learn a lot from our traditional nursery rhymes and songs. Many of these incorporate gesture and they are usually enjoyed and able to be extended. As an example, the well-known song, 'Here we go round the mulberry bush' incorporates many gestures: 'This is the way we wash our clothes . . .' and so on. And different actions can be added to the game: 'This is the way we comb our hair' or 'brush our teeth'. These actions can then be used on other occasions.

Choosing
A child can start to indicate his wants as soon as he can point, and shake his head, or nod. However, with only these gestures, his communication is still very limited – it is usually limited to things he can see.

The booklet called 'Ask for it' (p. 123) describes how you can help him to do this in words. Without words he may have difficulty in making himself understood and may become unhappy or frustrated.

As a child grows older, he will have more to communicate and more choices to make. It is important for him to exercise his choice, as decision-making is part of growing up, and also teaches a child about the world. If his speech is delayed for long, he should be given other methods of communication.

Use of pictures
A good idea is to prepare a set of pictures of your child's favourite toys. Let him match these pictures with the toys first and then put them into a box where he can get at them. Show him how he can 'ask' for a toy by bringing you its

picture, and then you exchange it for the toy. Make sure you also always name the picture, and get him to do the same if he can. If his articulation is poor, this picture game will reduce your uncertainty – you will know what he is trying to say.

If your child gets snacks or drinks during the day, prepare pictures of these. Encourage him to bring you the picture of what he wants when he is hungry or thirsty, e.g. a glass of milk. Also encourage him to name it if he can.

Going shopping
As children get older it is important to let them have some choice in what they wear or what toys you buy for them.

It is a good idea to cut pictures out of a mail order catalogue and let your child pick out the colour he likes for his new cardigan before you go to buy it. A child will be more co-operative if he has had some say in the matter.

This idea can be extended to sometimes giving the child a choice of outings or expeditions.

The look on your face
We get a great deal of information, not just from what people say, but from the look on their face while they say it, for example, when we know that somebody was pleased with the present we gave them. It is important in life to be able to pick up these signals. Handicapped children may find it difficult to interpret facial expressions. Most mothers help their baby quite naturally in this way – they smile when he smiles and perhaps pull a face in response to him. The more you can do in this way the better – exaggerate your facial expressions for him.

It is also a good idea to sit him in front of a mirror so that he can make faces at himself!

SECTION 2: LANGUAGE SKILLS

Introduction
Booklet 1: What's it called?
Booklet 2: In action
Booklet 3: Round about
Booklet 4: Putting two words together
Booklet 5: Ideas into words

INTRODUCTION

If your child is just starting to talk, or if he has not yet learnt to talk in proper sentences, you should find the booklets in this section useful. The Language Charts (p. 20) give an indication of the booklets you may find particularly appropriate.

This section is concerned with two important language skills, (1) learning the meaning of words and (2) putting words together in sentences.

The first three booklets deal with the learning of nouns, verbs and prepositions; the fourth booklet with the very important step of putting two words together in speech; and the fifth booklet with forming sentences.

Although these skills are very necessary in language, they should not be treated as ends in themselves. Children need to learn these skills mainly because they will help them to communicate better. Hence alongside these booklets you should also read the booklets in Section 3 (p. 119), where we describe games to encourage the use of language as a means of communication.

BOOKLET 1: WHAT'S IT CALLED?

In this booklet we suggest some games that you can play with your child to help him learn the names of objects, and to get him to use these words. These games are most suitable when the child is starting to talk, but they can be used later on to help him learn new words. Here are some hints to bear in mind:

Start by teaching the names of objects which have some meaning for the child. For example, drink, dinner or the names of his favourite toys – car, dolly, ball.

Choose words that are not too difficult to pronounce – remember we want to make it as easy as possible for the child. Also use short words like 'car' rather than 'tractor'.

Listen to the different sounds your child makes. Do any of these sound like words or parts of words? If so, it might be worth starting to teach these words.

Be consistent in the names you call the objects, otherwise you will confuse the child. Thus if the child's teddy is known by a name (e.g. Fred, Jane) then always use this, or always use the word 'teddy'. To use both will cause confusion.

When you come to start some of the games, it is best to begin with words that the child already knows. In this way he will catch on to the game more quickly.

Not all children like the same sort of games. Observe which particular game appeals most to your child and then use this. Remember when you start a new game it takes time for the child to get used to it – so don't give up too soon.

Finally, in helping the child to learn the names of objects, we want to help his understanding as well as his ability to speak the words. Most of the games can be used to do both, although some games will concentrate more on understanding (for example, the fetching or hiding games).

Here are some games you could play.

Fetching objects

Scatter some familiar toys around the floor, e.g. ball, car, dolly. Then ask the child to 'Bring me the *ball*!' At first you will have to point and even guide him to the toy, but when he brings it, make a great fuss – emphasising the name. 'Yes, it's the ball'. If you can get him to copy you saying the word, all the better! This game can be repeated until the child will bring the toy when you only say the word. At first the game can be very simple, perhaps with just the one toy on the floor, but you gradually make it more difficult for the child by adding more toys. This helps the child to realise that different things have different names. (This game can also be played with the child seated at a table or even lying down, as long as the toys are within reach.)

Hiding game

Have some small toys and at least two plastic cartons (old yoghurt cartons or plastic flower-pots) big enough to hide the toys under. Hide one of the toys under a carton and ask the child to fetch it, saying its name. When he finds it, make a fuss, emphasising the name of the object. If he copies you saying the word – well and good.

When the game is well established, introduce different toys. The game can be further extended by hiding two toys, one under each carton and asking the child to find one ('where's the ball?'). In this way you can be sure that he is properly understanding the words.

Posting-box

Make a hole in a cardboard box and place it upside down (see Figure 11). Then cut the bottom out of a paper cup and stick this into the hole (stops the child retrieving the objects).

1.   Collect some toys that the child likes to play with.
2.   Let the child post a toy which you know he can already

paper cup

Simple posting-box

Fig. 11

name. Make a game of you naming it and picking up the box to find it, saying 'Where's the ball?'.

3. When he has caught on to the idea of posting the toy – cover the hole with your hand and *don't* let him post the object until he has said its name. Then you can lift the box to find it as before.

4. Now try another toy, whose name the child doesn't know. Name this, getting the child to look at you as you name it. For example, put the toy close to your face. If he makes an attempt to copy you, even if it's not very good – give him the toy to post.

5. The game can be repeated until the child is saying the names of the toys correctly. You can then introduce other toys so the child realises that different objects have different names. This game could be played regularly for a short time each day; perhaps five minutes. You may well find that your child will begin to play it by himself.

Another posting game

With some children another type of posting-box can be useful. This time, divide the cardboard box into two halves with a piece of card that can be moved in and out (see Figure 12). This game is played in a similar way to the previous one;

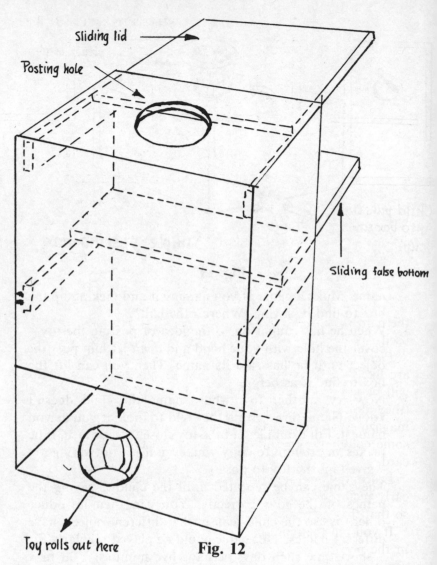

Sliding lid

Posting hole

Sliding false bottom

Toy rolls out here

Fig. 12

see Figure 13. This game further strengthens the link between the name and the actual object. It also helps the child to learn that saying things has a purpose; in this case it 'makes' the objects come back.

Pictures

Pictures are a very useful way of helping your child to learn

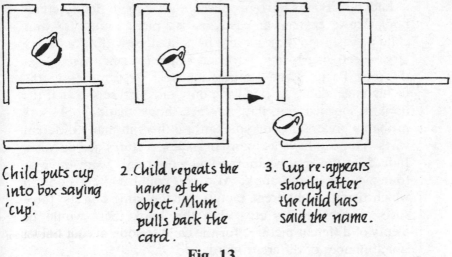

Child puts cup into box saying 'cup'.

2. Child repeats the name of the object. Mum pulls back the card.

3. Cup re-appears shortly after the child has said the name.

Fig. 13

the names of objects. Here are some of the ways they can be used.

Pictures of child's favourite toys or familiar objects – these are likely to be among the earliest pictures that your child will be able to name. You can have a go at drawing them (they don't have to be masterpieces!) or find pictures in magazines or catalogues that are similar. Even better, have some colour photographs taken and paste them on to stiff card.

Learning Development Aids have produced a set of sixteen early pictures on gummed paper (Early Language Stamps), so that they can be stuck on cards or into books.

If you put the pictures on to cards, you can then use them in the posting-box games, instead of the real objects. They can also be used in the fetching game: mum shows the child the picture of what she wants him to fetch.

Picture-books – these can be very useful in helping your child to learn the names of objects. But a word of warning: at first, only use a picture-book which has one object per page. Otherwise it will be difficult for him to link the name to the object.

Ladybird Books have produced a very good 'first' picture-book. However, you can easily make a picture-book for your child consisting of objects that he is familiar with. Fold some large sheets of paper in half and staple (or sew) together at the fold. Paste in the pictures, one per page but leave the facing page blank. In this way, only one picture shows if the book is opened out flat. In fact, home-made books are probably preferable, for you can use them in many different ways. You can have as many or as few pictures as you wish. Indeed, at the very beginning you would only want three or four pictures in the book. Also you could make a book in which there are different pictures of the same objects: three sorts of cups, chairs etc. With this book there would be plenty of different pictures for the child to look at, but only a small number of different words.

Here are two ways in which you can use picture-books.

Turning the pages – Your child will probably enjoy turning the pages of the book. However, before he's allowed to do this, get him to say the word. At first, you will have to say it clearly and any attempt to copy you is acceptable, and he turns the page. Later, only allow him to turn the page when he has said the word clearly.

Find me – In this game, the mum says the name of the object and the child has to find its picture. Ignore him until he turns up the right picture, then make a great fuss, repeating the name of the object – 'Yes, there's teddy'.

Scrap-books

Later on you could make up a number of different picture-books, each one having a particular theme, e.g. 'In the garden' or 'Bath-time'. For these, you could use pictures taken from magazines or catalogues stuck in a scrap-book. This will give your child plenty of practice at putting the right word to each of the objects.

Picture cubes

This can be a novel way of getting the child interested in pictures. Paste some pictures of familiar objects on to all the

sides of a small cardboard box or cube made out of polystyrene (see p. 68). Make this at least 6 × 6 × 6 in.

Show the child the picture and if he names it correctly, throw
the cube to him and let him play with it. Repeat this for the other
pictures until he can say all the names correctly by himself.

Picture roundabout

Another way in which you can use the picture cube is as a
'picture roundabout'. To do this, you stick a large knitting
needle through the middle of the cube (see p. 69). When you
hold the needle by its sharp end, you can then spin the cube,
making different pictures appear. Very little effort is required
to make the cube move. This is particularly useful with physically handicapped children who cannot move around easily,
or who find it difficult to hold a book.

At first, you can let the child spin the cube and when it stops,
you name the picture he sees. Later, you could let him spin the
cube only when he has made an attempt to name the picture.
You can also play the 'Find me' game: you ask him to find a
certain picture, ignore him until he does, then make a great fuss,
repeating the name of the object, 'Yes, there's the car'.

Finally, here are two games that can be used with older
children to help them learn new words.

Picture dominoes

These can either be made at home by sticking pictures on
match-boxes (see Figure 14), or bought (E.S.A. make a set).
Instead of numbers on the dominoes, there are pictures of
objects. The game is the same as ordinary dominoes: similar
pictures go together. This game not only helps the child to
look closely at the pictures so that he can match them, but it
helps him to learn their names, e.g. mum can say, 'You want
a knife – where's the knife?'. When it's mum's turn to go, he
can then tell mum what to look for.

Picture snap

You can also use a variation of the game 'snap'. Here all the
cards are pictures of objects, and when the same pictures are

Matchbox dominoes
Fig. 14

turned up, instead of calling 'snap', the child has to say the name of the object in order to win.

You can easily make your own set of cards by sticking pictures taken from magazines or catalogues on to postcards. Alternatively, you can buy sets of cards from E. J. Arnold and E.S.A.

Picture bingo, or Picture lotto
Prepare some large cards on which there are a number of different pictures, say six. Also have small cards with the same pictures but only one picture per card. One person is the 'caller' and holds up the small cards; one at a time. The players look to see if the picture is on their large card and if

so, they call out the name of the object. The first one to do so, gets the picture and places it on his large card. The first player to fill his card is the winner and calls Bingo! (You can buy sets of picture lotto from E.S.A. and Galt Toys.)

Final thoughts
Learning the names of objects is not easy, and we should give the child plenty of opportunity to learn through playing a variety of games. However, we also have to be sure that the child really has learnt the *meaning* of the words: for instance, the words 'cup' and 'ball', each refer to a whole range of objects, many of which look very different one from another. So if we are teaching words like this, we need to use a variety of different balls or cups in the games. Otherwise the child will think that only his cup is called 'cup'.

Also, it is best to use the words in a variety of short sentences. For example, if we continually say, 'It's a ball', the child may think that round objects are called 'It'saball'! We should use the word ball in different sentences – 'The ball's gone', 'Look, a ball', 'Kick the ball'.

BOOKLET 2: IN ACTION

This booklet is a continuation of the previous one, 'What's it called?', but this time we are going to be dealing with verbs rather than nouns. It is important that the child learns verbs, because without them all will never be able to talk in sentences. Yet it can be harder to learn verbs than nouns, since verbs refer to *actions* rather than to objects that can be seen and touched. With nouns, the child has to learn that an object, something he can see and feel, has its own name. But when it comes to verbs, he has to learn that many different objects can do the same thing, e.g. doll *sitting* on the table, cup *sitting* on the table, and that the *doing* has a name.

Here are some games you could play to help the child.

Doll play

At first sight, dolls might appear to be of use with girls only, but this is not so. Boys can equally well enjoy this sort of play. The advantage of dolls is that you can make them perform a lot of different actions – eating, sleeping, washing, kicking etc. (rag dolls are best for this). Indeed, you could build up a story with the dolls; 'getting ready for school' or 'the birthday party'. (You will find it useful to have some other toys – cups and saucers, chairs, beds etc.) The more you enter into the spirit of the game and use your imagination, the better. Some points to note:

(a) Have a number of dolls so that your child can copy you when you are playing with the dolls.

(b) When this sort of doll play is well established, you can then start concentrating on saying the verbs as you make, or he makes, the doll do the actions. (Remember to start off with only two or three simple verbs.)

(c) You can also help build up the child's understanding of the verbs by telling him, 'Make dolly eat (sit, kick etc.)'.

(d) Of course, alongside these activities you will be encouraging the child to say the verbs. For this, you could have him copy you (make sure he says the word in the right context though), or play a game when he tells you what to do with the doll. Do not make this into a lesson – he may not catch on at first but is likely to do so if he is enjoying the game.

(e) In the doll play it is important to have a number of different dolls, each with its own name, even if the names are only 'Mummy, baby or dolly'. We have to help the child realise that the same verb can be used with different 'people'. If we used only the one doll, he might think that the verb was another name for the doll.

(f) Also, we need to vary the context in which we say the verbs. Use a variety of short sentences; 'Dolly eat', 'Come on eat' or 'Eat it up'. Remember also to use the same form of the word in initial stages: i.e. KICK, not kickING or kickED.

Action games

Although doll play is a convenient way of introducing verbs, we also need to use the words with real people, and especially to apply them to the child's own actions. Here are some ways of applying new verbs in action:

Do this, do that – In this game the child has to copy the action you do. Include actions with simple verbs – eat, kick, sit, wash, walk. If the child is good at copying the actions, start using the verbs and get him to copy these.

Nursery rhymes – Many nursery rhymes have verbs in them. At first you can have the child mime the actions at the appropriate part of the rhyme, but you should soon start having him say the word, e.g. 'This is the way we *wash* our clothes'. With this sort of rhyme you can invent verses to suit yourself, e.g. 'comb our hair, climb the stairs etc.'

I must say – With some actions you can demand that the

child says the verb before he is allowed to do the action. The best example of this is the verb 'eat'. Here are some things you could do:

1. Put together some very small portions of his favourite food (sweets, crisps, nuts etc.); or if it is a meal-time, feed him with a spoon. Say firmly 'EAT', then you eat some food. Offer the child some; saying again, 'EAT' before he eats. Establish this as a routine.
2. Once the above is under way, you can make him copy you in saying 'EAT' before he can have the food. At first he should get the food for the slightest attempt – any sound will do. *Gradually* you can start demanding a better standard. Remember only to use small portions at a time: in that way he will get plenty of practice!
3. Once he can do this, you can start introducing another verb, e.g. 'drink' – but remember that this is a difficult word to say and do not expect it to be perfect.

It is possible to use this game with some other verbs; e.g. kick. The child has to say the word before he can kick the ball.

Giving commands – This game can be played in two ways. First, mum tells the child what to do. At first, the child may not actually do what you want him to but you can 'make' him do it, e.g. 'Johnny sit' as you push him (gently) into a chair.

Second, the child can tell the mum what to do. This is a good way of getting the child to use the verbs, and helping him to realise that language is worth using. In this form of the game you will have more control of the situation, for you only do the action when he has said the word. Also, if he uses the wrong word, you can do the 'wrong' action, e.g. if he is pointing to you to sit down and says 'kick' – then you kick. He will then realise that different actions have different names. You can get the child to play this game by at first having two adults or another child to demonstrate, e.g. mum tells dad what to do, then gets the child to copy her.

Pictures

Just as pictures are useful when learning nouns, they can also be used with verbs: often we forget this, and concentrate too much on nouns. Here are some ways in which you can use pictures to teach verbs.

1. When looking at pictures of objects, as well as asking the name ask what we do with it. (If need be you can mime the action.) For this you may need to make a special book of objects which we use for everyday things, e.g. soap, hammer, spoon, comb. If people occur in the pictures you can ask what they are doing (again mime the action, or have the child mime it). Finally, you can have the child pretend to do actions associated with objects, e.g. with a sweet the child can pretend to eat it; with a comb he can pretend to comb his hair.

2. Make a picture-book of people doing different things. If you can use the same 'person' throughout, all the better. (The 'person' could be a teddy bear, or the child's favourite doll, etc.) As the child looks at the pictures, have him tell you what the person is doing.

    These pictures need not be in the form of a book. For example, it might be more interesting for the child if you made a 'television' screen out of an old cardboard box. Draw or stick the pictures on to a long roll of paper. Attach this to two round pieces of wood (thick knitting needles would do), which are pushed through the sides of the box (see Figure 15). You can then make each picture appear on the telly by turning the knitting needles ('the knobs'). In time, the child could learn to do this by himself, being allowed to turn the knob only once he has said the verb.

    Alternatively, you can keep a series of 'verb flash cards'. On each card have a person doing a different action. When you show a card the child has to do the action, e.g. 'kick'. After a time when he starts doing the actions quite well, you can ask him what he is doing (see Figure 16). Phillip &

Fig. 15

Fig. 16

Tacey produce a set of 'Things-We-do' Pictorial Gummed stamps which you could use here.

Moving pictures – The disadvantage of pictures when it comes to verbs is that they don't move – there's no action with them. To overcome this you can make pictures with moving parts. This means that you can have the person in the picture do the action as you say the verb. For example, draw a picture on stiff card of your child's favourite doll (it's better to have more than one picture for each action). Cut out another piece of card for the moving part, i.e. the arm for the verb 'EAT'. Attach this to the drawing using a brass paper-fastener (see Figure 17) – obtainable from stationers.

This is the simplest sort of moving picture, but the disadvantage is that the child may find it difficult to operate. For more elaborate pictures, you could attach a strip of card behind the picture on to the same clip as the moving part, so that when the strip is pulled the arm moves. This sort of

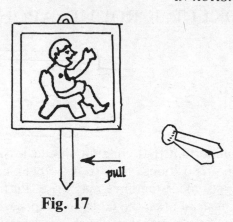

Fig. 17

picture could be more useful if attached to a wall than if the child is allowed to hold it (see Figure 17).

Drawing
You don't have to be an artist to play this game, as simple stick figures will suffice. You can draw the man doing different actions, then get the child to mime it and say what he's doing. Alternatively, you can have the child tell you what to draw.

Everyday activities
Often on outings, we point out objects for the children, but we tend to overlook actions. Remember to draw attention to something happening – e.g. look at the man *running* . . . at the lady *pushing* the pram etc. Encourage him to tell you what people are doing by asking questions such as, 'What's that man doing?'

BOOKLET 3: ROUND ABOUT

It is important that children should learn to distinguish between prepositions, and to use them correctly. Otherwise many misunderstandings may arise. Putting a cup *under* the table, instead of *on* the table, may appear as naughtiness, but it may simply reflect a lack of understanding of the words ON and UNDER.

Although it is important to help children towards an understanding of these words, we must choose our time carefully. A child has to have reached a certain stage of maturity in his play before he is ready for prepositions.

At first, he will be able to play with only one object at a time; then later with two objects together, although only in a simple way. He may be able to hit a drum with a stick; or a ball with a bat; or to feed a doll. Later, through experience and encouragement, he will begin to appreciate more complex relationships. For instance, he will realise that many different things can be done with a box and some bricks. All the bricks can be *in* the box, or he can tip them all out together. He can even turn the box upside-down and place his bricks on the box; or, if he is careful, perch the box on the bricks. He can hide them under the box; or behind the box; or arrange them in front.

These games may appear boring and repetitious to us, but through them a child is learning about relationships between objects.

It is also very important that the child experiences these relationships himself, e.g. being *in* a box, *under* the bed-clothes, *behind* a chair etc. Obviously with active children this is no problem, but with physically handicapped children we may have to ensure that they do experience being in different situations. This will mean bringing the experiences to them, e.g. putting them in a large box, putting the box on top of them etc.

When the child starts to show an interest in this type of play or in playing with objects as described above, then you can start introducing the appropriate prepositions. At first, you should use only two prepositions at the most and, possibly contrasting ones, such as *in* and *out*, or *up* and *down*, or *on* and *under*.

However, the main thing at this stage is to provide many different objects which can be played with in this way. You should join in the play and make sure your child hears the correct word at the right time; *in* the box, *under* the box, *on* the table, *on* your head, *out* of the box, *in front* of the box, *behind* the box and so on.

Up and *down* can be introduced fairly early, in boisterous play, when one is swinging a child up and down in one's arms. As you lift him up, say 'UP'.

Dropping-in games
Collect a variety of containers and different things to put inside them. Here are a few suggestions:

Containers – plastic buckets, yoghurt cartons, plastic flower pots, margarine containers, squeezy bottles, coffee tins etc.

Fillers – bricks, wooden beads, shells, acorns, nuts, pebbles.

If possible, sand and water play should also be included.

The earliest games consist only of taking an interest, and perhaps taking turns, in putting things into a container and saying 'IN it goes!' as it drops to the bottom. You may have to persevere for some time before your child will echo your 'IN it goes!' or 'IN', but sometimes you can encourage him by seeming to be forgetful and when it is your turn, only holding the objects above the container without putting them in. Children often speak more when slightly frustrated.

Many games similar to the one above can be played at bath-time. Toy ducks, for instance, make a nice splash when dropped in the water.

Posting-boxes – Children like posting objects through slits or holes, and many varieties of posting-boxes can be bought. In fact suitable holes can be made in any strong box for objects to be posted through (see p. 83); or the hole in an up-turned flower-pot can be used for posting small objects. As in the previous game, when the child posts an object into the box, he should say, 'IN' or 'IN it goes'.

A posting-box with a false bottom and a sliding lid is useful for this game too (see 84). You can slide the lids so that the child can get the object into the box only when he has said 'IN', and he has to say 'OUT' before you release the object again.

This game can be developed in many different ways. Once he can say 'in' or 'out' correctly, you can post a variety of objects into the box and release the lid only when he has named the object and said 'in', i.e. 'car in', 'shoe in' and so on. Or you can develop it into a memory game so that he has to tell you first all the objects that have gone in, i.e. 'shoe, car and ball IN' and then all the objects as they came out, i.e. 'shoe, car and ball OUT!'

Hiding Games

Many different hiding games can be used to teach children about the relative positions of objects and to help them speak about them. A doll or teddy who keeps hiding is useful, and then you both look where he has gone. At first you will probably have to tell the child, 'Look, he's *on* the clock!' 'He's *under* the rug!' 'He's *in* the bed' etc. Gradually encourage the child to tell **you**.

Hunt the thimble – This is played like the traditional game (any small object can be hidden), except that the child is given a clue as to the whereabouts of the thimble – 'It's *under* the rug', '*On* the clock', '*Behind* the piano' and so on.

When the child is fairly adept at the game, let him hide the thimble and tell you where it is.

Through the tunnel – The idea of one object passing through another is quite difficult, and needs plenty of practice. It is a good idea to make several tunnels out of halves of cardboard tubes or from papier maché. These should be big enough to allow toy cars, trains etc. to be pulled through them. Again you should join in the play so that the child learns the right word at the right moment and gets the idea 'Where's the train?' – 'It's going *through* the tunnel' Other prepositions come into this game; the train goes IN at one end and OUT the other.

Your child may like threading wooden beads on to a lace or threading cotton reels. When you are showing him how to do this, you can make a ritual of saying '*In* it goes – *through* the bead – *out* it comes'.

Naughty cat – Cut out or draw pictures of furniture or objects around the house and make a separate picture of a cat (or child's favourite animal), cut out and mount on card (see Figure 18, which you could trace).

Tell a story about this naughty cat, who is always jumping on to furniture and going where he should not go. He should stay IN his basket or ON the rug. As you tell the story, move the cat around and then turn to it and suddenly tell it off! 'You *naughty* cat, you're ON the television! Get down!' Move the cat on to the floor, saying 'Good cat, stay ON the floor'. This game may sound infantile when described, but it usually goes down well and does help to teach prepositions.

This game can equally well be played with doll's furniture and a model animal.

Cowboys and Indians – As well as appreciating positions of objects a child needs to appreciate his own position in space, and this game should help. First you must prepare the room or garden, and tell the child, or children, what the furniture represents; a large box with open ends is a tunnel, an upturned umbrella could be a tree, the gap between the lines on the tiles a river, stools could be rocks and a blanket shrubs

The naughty cat

Fig. 18

etc. As you tell a dramatic story the children carry out the actions. It starts to rain and they must shelter *under* the tree, the cowboys are after them and they must cross *over* the river to the other side and hide *behind* the rocks, or they must go *through* the tunnel and climb on top of the rocks to signal to their friends, and so on. The number of actions and positions included can be varied, with only a few the first time, but as the child gets used to the game, the number can be increased. Later, he can tell you and the other children what to do.

Mouse book
This is a way in which you can use pictures to help your child learn prepositions. The idea is for the child to 'hunt' the mouse. Here's what you do. Paste a picture of an item of furniture on each page of a scrap-book (mail-order catalogues are a useful source of pictures). Also on each page have a picture of a mouse. Put it in a different position each

time, e.g. on the bed, under the chair, sometimes in full view, sometimes half-hidden. (You could make a cardboard template of the mouse, by tracing it on to card.) You need then only draw round this to get the outline of the mouse, which you can colour in (see Figure 19).

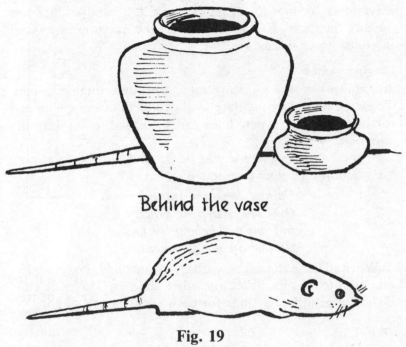

Behind the vase

Fig. 19

As you look at the book with your child, talk about the mouse: wonder where he can be and exclaim; 'There he is, *behind* the stove', '*under* the chair', 'in *front* of the telly', and so on.

As you use the book, gradually increase the time before you find the mouse so that the child has time to get there first and tell you where the mouse is. Sometimes you should get it wrong so that he has a chance to correct you.

Picture-books
Any picture-book can be used to help your child use prepositions. As you turn the pages ask questions: 'Where's the

boy?' for instance. At first you may have to give the answer yourself! 'The boy's behind the door.' If your child has difficulty in responding, you can help him gradually. You begin by saying 'The boy's behind . . .' and let him complete the sentence. Show your pleasure when he does. Then gradually leave more for him to say – 'The boy's . . .' and let him add 'behind the door'. Your aim is to get the questions answered in complete sentences.

Singing games

An enjoyable way of learning is through singing games. These are best played with several people but can be modified for one child. Also new lines can be added in the learning situation.

A good singing game would be 'In and out the windows'. New action lines could be added:

> *Up and down the staircase,*
> *Over and under the bridges,*
> *In front and behind the houses,*
> *On and off the pavement.*

When playing this game with only one child, boxes, chairs etc. need to be substituted for other children. Have the child do the appropriate actions for each verse as you sing it.

BOOKLET 4: PUTTING TWO WORDS TOGETHER

It is a very important landmark in the child's language development when he starts to speak two words together, for this marks the start of talking in sentences. It also means that the child is able to communicate more clearly. When the child is only using one word, we have to 'guess' at what he is trying to say. But if the child starts to use two words, we have a better idea of what he is talking about.

There is a danger, especially with handicapped children, in keeping on encouraging them to use one word. We are so pleased that they have started to talk that we accept one word from them over and over again – we, after all, know what they mean. Instead we should soon be encouraging the child to express himself more clearly. You could start encouraging your child to use two words if:

1. you have noted a few instances of the child starting to link words together by himself;
2. the child is using correctly a fairly large number of single words (around 30–50 different words).

Remember though, that these are only rough guidelines, that children vary a lot, and that there is a danger of confusing the child if you push him on too fast.

Many of the games in this booklet have already been mentioned in previous booklets, particularly those concerned with the learning of nouns ('What's it called?') and the learning of verbs ('In action'). This time however the games are used with a different purpose in mind, so if you have already used some of these games to teach either nouns or verbs, you may have to give the child time to catch on to the new idea.

Posting-box

Make a hole in a cardboard box and place it upside down (see p. 83).

1.   Collect together a number of small toys which the child can name correctly, e.g. ball, cup, doll etc. It's best to have about ten such toys, but use only five at first, keeping the other five for later – see point four below.

The child should also be able to say at least one extra word such as 'gone, bye-bye or gimme', for during the game one of these words will be linked with a noun to make two words – 'Ball gone', 'Cup gone'. Choose a word which your child is already using, or one that he finds easiest to say. Then only use this word throughout the game.

2.   Play a posting game of **you** putting the toys into the hole and saying 'Ball gone' or 'Bye-bye ball'.

3.   Give the child a turn at posting the toys, but do not let him post the toy until he has said at least one of the words. Then let him lift the box to find the toy. When he has got into the way of the game, let him post the toy only when he attempts to say two words. At first you will have to model this for him so that he can copy you, but with practice he should be able to use the two words by himself.

4.   You can find out how well your child has caught on to the two-word idea by introducing the toys which you know he can name, but which have never been used in the game (see point one). Now, as he is playing the game with the 'old' toys, introduce these new toys but do **not** give him a model, i.e. you must not say 'cup gone'. We want to see if he will say this by himself. If he does, he has caught on to the idea, if he doesn't, then carry on the game with the 'old' toys, and try the 'new' toys later. In time he will catch on.

Posting-box – Mark two

Another type of posting-box can be useful for teaching different sorts of two-word sentences, especially those with words such as 'give me, want, come on' (see p. 84).

This time, divide the cardboard box into two halves with a piece of card that can be moved in and out – this is played in a similar manner to the other game.

1. Select a number of toys that you know the child can name but leave some to one side for a later stage of the game. The child should also be able to say one word like 'want, gimme'. Choose one which your child is already using, or one that he finds easiest to say. Use this word throughout the game.

2. Show him how to play the game by posting one of the objects, pausing, then saying, 'Want ball' or 'Give me ball'. Immediately after you have said it, make the object re-appear by pulling back the card.

3. Have the child play the game, but do not make the toy re-appear until he has said at least one of the words. You can start demanding a higher standard as he gets used to the game. Only make the toy re-appear when he attempts to say two words. You should model this for him so that he can copy you, but in time the child should be able to use the words by himself.

4. You can find out how well your child has caught on to the idea of two words by introducing some toys which you know he can name, but which have never been used in the game. Now when he is playing the game with the 'old' toys, introduce the new toys but do **not** give him a model for these, i.e. you must **not** say 'want cup'. The idea is to see if he will do this on his own. If he doesn't, carry on with the 'old' toys, then have another try with the new toys later.

Throughout the games it is important to keep using the same action word, i.e. 'gone', 'want' etc. Once you have chosen the word, stick to it until you are sure the child has learnt the idea of linking it with nouns.

Give-me game
Another useful way to teach two-word sentences with words

such as 'give me' or 'want', is the following game. Collect together a number of small objects – toy car, comb, ball etc. Line these along one side of a narrow table. You sit on one side of this; the child sits on the opposite side facing you. All the child has to do, is simply ask for the object he wants, e.g. 'Gimme car'. At first it's best to have two adults, e.g. mum sits with the child and dad passes over the objects. Mum can then say to dad, 'Give me car', thus showing the child what to do. If you do this, the child will quickly catch on to the game. At first give him the object if he makes any attempt at saying 'Give me', but gradually become more strict so that he has to say the name of the object as well.

When all the objects have been passed over to the child, the roles are then reversed. The adult then has to ask the child for each object. This not only gives the child further examples of how to ask for the objects but it is an opportunity for you to check on his understanding of nouns, i.e. he reaches straight for the car when you ask for it.

Although this game doesn't sound very exciting, children do enjoy it. You can also develop it into playing 'shops'; with one of you as the customer and the other the shop-keeper.

It's here

Another type of two-word sentence involves words like 'here' or 'there'. These sentences give the location of objects, e.g. 'Ball here' or 'Chair there'. This game will help your child to learn this sort of sentence. Spread out a variety of objects on a large table or over the floor. Then make a play of hiding your eyes and asking, 'Where's the ball?' etc. The child then has to find it for you and say, 'Ball here', before you open your eyes. Again having two adults playing the game first, is the best way of showing your child how the game is played.

Doll play

This can be a useful way of helping the child to use two words, one of which is a verb. The game, by the way, can equally well be played with boys or girls.

1.   Have a number of rag dolls (three maybe) each having a

different appearance and called by a different name, even if it's only 'baby', 'mummy' or 'dolly'.

2. Build up a pretend situation with the dolls: make them do various actions such as walking, eating, sitting etc. (It's useful to have some other toys – such as chairs, cups, spoons etc – for this.) You can build up a story around the dolls, 'Going to school' for instance, and really enter into the spirit of the game. Don't make it into a lesson, be as natural as possible; make it enjoyable for the child and enjoy it yourself!

3. Encourage the child to copy your play with the dolls. When he is making the dolls do the actions, you can start concentrating on saying the name of the doll and the verb, i.e. 'Mummy eat, Baby kick, Dolly sit' etc. You can say this before **you** make the doll do an action, as if you were giving it a command. Also if the child makes the doll do an action, you can say 'Baby eat' etc. You can also help build up the child's understanding of the words by having him do particular actions with certain dolls, e.g. saying to him 'Now mummy eat'.

4. Encourage him to use the two words, either by getting him to copy you saying the two words (see above), or else by playing a game where he has to tell you what to do with the doll.

5. Later, you can also use the doll play for sentences which have a verb and an object, e.g. 'Eat sweet (apple, biscuit etc.)' or 'Sit chair (table, bed etc.)'. In the doll play, you can make the doll sit on the chair, bed, table, and as you do, say the appropriate sentence.

Giving commands

This is a good way of getting the child to use two words and is a game in which both mum and dad can join. The idea is for the child to tell mum or dad to do a particular action, i.e. to say 'Mummy sit' or 'Daddy kick'. At first, mum might have to tell dad what to do and have the child copy her. When the child has caught on he can give the commands, but remember you should only do the action if he has said **two** words. Also you should do exactly what he says. If he points to mum to sit down but says 'Daddy kick', then dad should do just that!

Pictures

Pictures can also be very useful in helping your child to learn two-word sentences, especially when used alongside some of the games suggested. Here are some examples:

1. *Picture gone!* – Make a picture-book of some of the child's toys but have only one toy per page **and** a blank page between each picture. When looking through the book with the child, as you turn the page you can say 'Ball gone' or 'Bye-bye ball' – and have the blank page showing. The child can copy you saying this. The game can be extended into the child having to say 'Ball gone' etc. before you turn (or he is allowed to turn) the page over. The game can be used alongside the posting-box game.

2. *Picture-books* – You can use picture-books which have one object per page in a variety of ways. For example, in a variation of the 'It's here' game (p. 106), you can hide your eyes until the child turns up the right page and says 'Ball here'. Alternatively, you can introduce the picture-book into the doll play and have the doll looking at the pictures. You can make the doll do something with the object shown, e.g. 'eat' the sweet or 'sit' on the chair. As you do this say, 'Eat sweet' etc.

3. *Action pictures* – These pictures can be used in conjunction with the doll play. Draw some pictures of the rag dolls doing various actions. Have the child name these ('Dolly kick' etc.), perhaps starting with you saying the words so that he can copy you (see p. 58).

These pictures need not be in the form of a book. For example it might be more interesting for the child if you make a 'TV screen' (see p. 94). Stick the pictures to a long roll of paper. Attach the end of this to wooden rods (thick knitting needles might do) which have been placed through

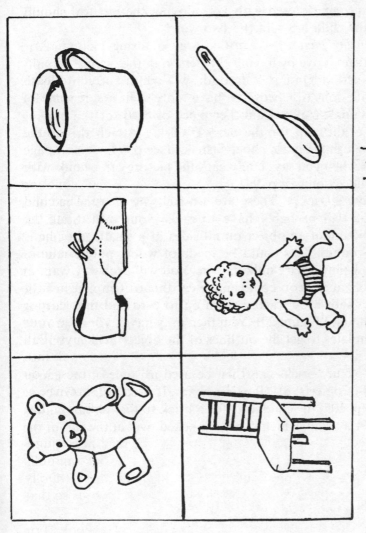

Pictures for use on picture bricks

Fig. 20

the card television 'frame'. Now as you turn the 'knobs' at the side, the pictures will appear on the screen. Once again the game can be used with you moving the picture, or only when the child has said the two words.

4. *Moving pictures* – Another way of using pictures is to make them move by having the person in the picture actually do the action. On a stiff card, draw a picture of your child's favourite dolls (it's better to have more than one picture for each action). Cut out another piece of card for the moving part, i.e. the arm for the verb EAT . . . Attach this to the drawing using a brass paper-fastener (see p. 94).

Now when you say 'Dolly eat', the picture can be moved to show the action (see p. 94).

5. *Picture bricks* – These are a novel way of using pictures and you will probably have to make your own. Stick the *same* picture of an object on all sides of a small cube (e.g. 2 ins all round). This could be made of wood, polystyrene or from a ½-pint square milk carton. You will probably want at least six cubes. You could make cardboard templates of the pictures shown by tracing them on to card and then cutting them out (see Figure 20). You then only have to draw around the templates to get the outlines of the objects which you can colour in.

The picture bricks can then be used in some of the games instead of objects, e.g. Posting-boxes. If used in the 'Give-me game' (p. 105) the child asks for a brick so that he can build a tower or a 'wall', which can be knocked over at the end of the game.

BOOKLET 5: IDEAS INTO WORDS

Before a child can speak in sentences as adults do, he has to have mastered a great many skills. He will not be able to master all these skills at once, and so we see his language gradually developing from the babbling stage to the one-word stage until he starts experimenting with putting two words together: 'dinner gone', 'nice pussy', 'bye-bye daddy'.

It is not until he has mastered this stage that he will be able to go on to the next stage. He will then begin to put several words together and to convey a great deal of meaning without using grammatically correct sentences. At this stage his language reminds us of the kind of language we use when we are sending a telegram – we leave out as many words as we can and still make ourselves understood. For example, we may say: 'Arriving Waterloo Monday, noon'. Children do the same kind of thing, 'Mummy, dog gone!' They put in enough words to convey the content of their thought but leave out what we call 'function' words – that is words which have no meaning on their own but help to make a sentence clearer – like 'the', 'a', 'because', 'as' and so on.

If your child knows many words and is putting two and three words together, here are some games you can play to help him structure longer and more correct sentences.

Doll play

You can extend the doll play which we described in the previous booklet (see p. 106) to help your child make three-word sentences, such as 'Dolly sit chair' or 'Teddy eat sweet'. In fact these sentences are a combination of the two types of utterances mentioned in that booklet, i.e. 'Dolly sit' and 'Sit chair' . . . the three-word sentence contains both ideas. Once your child is capable of using these two-word sentences in doll play, you can start to introduce the three-word sentences when playing with the dolls, and have him do so too.

Picture split

This game involves a special type of picture-book (which you will have to make for yourself) in which each page is cut in half, so that the top and bottom parts can be turned separately. On the 'top' pages of the book, paste pictures of people, e.g. photographs of the child, mum, dad etc., or pictures of some of the dolls used in the doll play, e.g. teddy. On the 'bottom' pages, put pictures of objects which can all go with the same verb: for example, sweets, biscuit, ice-cream, apple can go with the verb 'eat' (see Figure 21). By now,

Picture split

Fig. 21

you've probably guessed how to use the book: by combining any person in a sentence with any object, so that a lot of different sentences can be used to describe the same basic set of pictures, e.g. 'Mum (dad, baby, teddy) eat sweet (biscuit, ice-cream, apple)' – there are sixteen possibilities in that example alone!

With this sort of picture-book, you can either have your child say the appropriate sentence as you (or he) turn the pages; or alternatively, you can say, 'Show me teddy eating ice-cream' and he has to find the right pictures.

It is a good idea to use a ring folder to hold the pictures (these are obtainable at most stationers). In this way you will be able, for instance, to replace the objects if you wish to, but leave the pictures of the people. You can then make up different sets of pictures, so that you can make sentences with different verbs. For example, pictures of chair, bed, stool, table, to go with the word 'sit', or car, bus, bike, lorry, pram to go with the word 'go', will give sentences such as 'Mum sit chair' or 'Dad go pram'!

Giving commands

You can also extend the 'Giving commands' game which we mentioned in the previous booklet (see p. 107), to include three-word sentences. Here all the family can join in: mum, dad, brothers, sisters etc. Each person takes a turn to be 'in charge' and to tell the others what to do. The command takes the form of a three-word sentence, e.g. 'Mum sit (on the) chair', 'Dad kick (the) ball', 'Aunty comb (your) hair'. You say the complete sentence, perhaps emphasising the three main words. However, when it's your child's turn concentrate on having him say these three words. At first he will need help and you can prompt him by saying part of the command, 'Daddy . . . sit . . .'.

In this game the child hears lots of examples of three-word sentences and he has a real incentive to use them himself, because when he does, people obey him.

Later on, when he has grasped the idea of three-word sentences, you can make the game harder for him by following his commands only when he has said the full sentence, putting all the words in: e.g. 'Daddy sit *on the* floor'.

Action pictures

Collect a series of pictures of people doing things: skipping, singing, playing the guitar, skating, riding, swimming, eating and so on. To play this game, you hold up one picture at a time, and your child first mimes the action, and then tells you what he is doing: 'I'm swimming'. Then get him to tell you what the boy is doing: 'The boy is swimming'. If he can do this, he is ready to go on to harder sentences.

For these you could prepare a second set of pictures to go with the first. For example, a picture of skipping and a rope on its own, a picture of someone playing a guitar and a guitar on its own, a boy eating and some jelly on its own. These could be on separate cards or on the back of the first cards (see Figure 22). When your child has said, 'The boy is eating', you turn the card over suddenly and say 'the jelly' very quickly. Next time see if he will remember and be able to say 'The boy is eating the jelly' without prompting. If not, prompt him first with the picture and then by saying it yourself.

Sentence strips

You may despair of your child being able to speak in sentences: even if he tries to imitate you he can often parrot only the end of the sentence. These sentence strips will help (see Figure 23).

Cut out a strip of paper or thin card about 3 ins wide and 3 ft long. Prepare a card 5 ins wide and 18 ins long and cut two slits in the card, as shown. Draw a picture of a pig, or cat or dog, on the long strip and a sty or house on the short strip. Thread the long strip through the slits and show the child how to make the pig appear, and then run along and disappear into the sty.

Do this in slow motion so that your words are in time with the action – 'The pig ... runs ... into the sty'. Encourage

Action pictures
Fig. 22

The pig runs into the sty

The bear runs into the wood
Sentence strips

Fig. 23

your child to repeat this, but do not let the pig move on until the appropriate words have been said. You could then make several more moving picture strips.

Stories

It is a good thing to start telling your child stories quite early. The first stories will be **very** short and you may have to make them up yourself. Later, repetitive folk tales are very useful. 'The gingerbread man' is a good one to choose, or 'The three bears' and 'The little red hen'. As your child begins to enjoy hearing the stories over and over again, you should start encouraging him to repeat a few words. For instance, in 'The Gingerbread Man' the words 'Run, run as fast as you can, you can't catch me, I'm the Gingerbread man', are constantly repeated. At first you will have to say these words every time. Then you can say them but leave out the last word – '. . . you can't catch me, I'm the Gingerbread . . .', and wait for your child to say 'man' and show you are pleased when he does. As soon as he can do this well every time, you could start leaving out two words. '. . . you can't catch me, I'm the . . .'. You do not make a fuss of him until he has said them both. Eventually you should be able to get him saying the whole sentence. Also, encourage him to re-tell bits of the story from the book, with you as the listener.

Drawing

Drawing can be used to create a situation for the child to talk about. It will be quite natural to draw a house and say such things as 'I wonder who lives in this room?' (as you put in the windows). 'Oh, do you think it's Aunt Mary? What do you think she's doing now?' Then, rather than correct your child's grammar, listen to what he says and add a bit more 'I guess she's knitting a pullover for Sid', and so on.

Draw-a-story

In another way, drawing can help a child to put words together in longer sentences. On a large sheet of paper or on a blackboard, first draw a figure of a boy or girl, and then,

scattered over the paper, draw several objects – like a tree
with fallen apples and a basket, and a dog chasing a cat. Let
your child name the objects of the picture and the character
(e.g. Mary). Then ask him to tell you a story about Mary;
point to Mary and then point to the tree, the basket and the
apples and possibly the dog and the cat if he dries up. Main-
tain your interest in the story, 'What did Mary do next when
she had put the apples in the basket?' (see Figure 24).

Draw a story
Fig. 24

Final thoughts

Questions – If we want to encourage a child to talk in sentences, or to use longer phrases, we should pay attention to the kind of questions we ask. We may find that we are asking the kind of questions which call only for one-word answers, e.g. 'What's that?' (pointing to a picture). 'What colour is it?' 'How many legs has it got?' Although it is much harder to think of questions which need longer answers, they are very important in getting your child to speak in sentences. For instance, we might say 'I wonder what daddy is doing just now . . .?'

It is much harder to answer this kind of question with only one word!

Expanding sentences – Do not be worried if your child doesn't use proper sentences, with words like 'the' or 'is' in them. The skill will come if you continue to give him clear examples of proper sentences, and show an interest in what he says. This tactic will probably be much more effective than having him copy you saying proper sentences, in which you emphasise what are really the unimportant words, e.g. '*The* man *is* driving *the* car'.

SECTION 3: USING LANGUAGE TO COMMUNICATE

INTRODUCTION

The emphasis in this section is on games and activities designed to help children communicate with others through language. This is something you should encourage from an early age, even before the child has mastered all the language skills. For after all, the most important thing in communication is *what* you say and not how you say it.

You will probably find the booklets in this section most useful if your child has started to talk, whether it is in proper sentences or only in single words. However, even if your child is not yet talking you should find some parts helpful, especially Booklet 1.

Children learn a great deal of language simply because their parents talk to them. Hence the first booklet in this section suggests ways in which you can use everyday activities as talking points with your child.

The second booklet deals with games and activities that will encourage the child to use language in communication. Handicapped children often find they don't need to use language, simply because their parents do everything for them: they anticipate the child's needs and wishes. You must beware of doing this with your child. If you want him to speak well, you should make it worthwhile for him to use language.

Finally, children should be encouraged to communicate with each other. It is very easy to overlook this with handicapped children, and yet it is a very necessary part of their development. The third booklet suggests games to encourage communication between children.

BOOKLET 1: WHAT SHALL WE DO NOW?

Talking to your child

Children model themselves on their mums and dads a great deal. This is often the way they learn to do things, so if mums and dads don't give them this example, it will be harder for them to learn. This is especially so when it comes to the learning of language. Not only do children need to hear other people talking but they need people to talk *to* them.

However, as you talk to your child remember that he will not be able to understand all that you say. You can help him to understand more if you talk clearly and in simple sentences about things which are actually happening. Also it is worth repeating some sentences, maybe with slight variations, and to emphasise certain words: e.g. (as you are doing the washing up) 'Now for the plates. First the big plates. The plates are in the water. Clean the plates.' Of course, as your child's language develops, you can use longer sentences.

Remember also to shut up sometimes! It is important that your child has a chance to say something, even if it is only to copy what you said.

And don't be put off by all these cautions – the main thing is that you should talk to your child. This booklet describes how you can use everyday activities as talking points with your child.

Housework

If you are working around the house and your child is with you, simply talk out loud about what it is you are doing – making the bed, peeling potatoes or laying the table. You can name the things you're using, ask questions, get him to find you things and so on. In some ways it's rather like giving a B.B.C. commentary! The child may take no notice but at least he will be hearing somebody speaking.

You can develop this sort of game by making scrap-books which show pictures of different household activities. (Mail-order catalogues or colour magazines come in useful here.) Keep one page of the book for each activity, e.g. you can have one page for 'washing-up' – showing sink, basin, washing-up liquid, cups, saucers. You can use the book to 'relive' the activities the child has watched you doing.

An important way in which you can help your child's language (and help yourself!) is to get the child to fetch things for you. At first you will probably have to point out what you want and even guide him to the object, but when he brings it, make a great fuss. In time you can get him to fetch the things by simply telling him where they are, e.g. 'It's over by the chair, no, not that one, the big chair . . .' If he can't find it, then show him and repeat again, 'you see, it's near the big chair'.

As he learns to do these tasks, you can then get him to fetch things from other rooms, and to bring more than one object.

Shopping

When outside with the child you can give the same sort of running commentary as for the household tasks – pointing out new things (as well as the familiar things), asking questions. But the occasional outing you can build up into a real event. This will help the child to participate actively, and counter any tendency he may have to lose interest and become a merely passive onlooker. For example, before leaving home you can talk about what you are going to do, e.g. 'We're going to post this letter, buy a stamp, lick it, then put it on the letter.' When you return home, you can help the child relive the activity by making a scrap-book, or by using model houses, shops and people or by having a pretend game. Indeed, with familiar activities you could use the models or play the pretend game before going, and then let the child have a part in the actual buying – he could ask for the bread or meat.

Special treats

Special treats such as going on holiday or to a party, riding on a train, celebrating bonfire night are not only exciting for the child but they can be a great aid in developing his language. Before any special treat, talk about it with the child, perhaps using pictures or playing a pretend game. Then afterwards you can relive the occasion by making a scrap-book of souvenirs.

Story book

Telling your child stories or nursery rhymes is another great help to his language development. Here are some ways in which rhymes or stories can be used:

If the story or nursery rhyme is accompanied by pictures, this will help the child to grasp the meaning of the language. Ladybird story books are particularly useful here, as they have a picture on each page.

You can extend the story through the pictures – using them as talking-points with the child. You needn't always keep precisely to the story.

If it's a familiar story, instead of you telling it to the child, get him to tell the whole or part of it to you. Stories which have a sentence that is repeated are useful for this, e.g. in the story of the Gingerbread man (Ladybird) there's a sentence that is repeated several times: 'Run, run as fast as you can, you can't catch me, I'm the Gingerbread man'. The child can 'tell' this part of the story. Later he can be encouraged to retell the story from the pictures.

Although you will obviously want to buy some story books for your child, it is also worth joining your local library, which probably stocks a wide range of children's books. A library gives your child access to a greater variety of stories than you can provide, and if he doesn't like a particular book, you can just return it: no money is wasted.

Remember also to let him have a say in choosing his books, so take him along to the library with you.

Picking the right story

Of course the child will not be interested in a story if it's too complicated for him. We have to be careful in the stories we select. The earliest stories you could use might have only one character (you can use the child's name, for this often catches the interest) doing a number of different things – like getting out of bed, washing, dressing then having breakfast. One of the scrap-books suggested in the earlier games might be your story book! (e.g. the washing-up book could be used for a story about a broken plate.) As the child's language progresses, you can move on to more complicated stories.

Nursery Rhymes

Although the child will enjoy listening to nursery rhymes, he should be encouraged to join in, even though he only says jargon. This will give him practice at speech rhythms. He can also join in the actions, but you can also get him saying parts of the rhyme, for example, by collecting some toys or objects that occur in the rhyme (e.g. in 'Hickory, Dickory, Dock' you could have a mouse and a clock). When saying the rhyme, pause when you come to these words, then produce the toy from behind your back and say dramatically *MOUSE*. Continue on to the next word (clock) and do the same thing. Later, produce the toy only when the child *says* the word. In this way he will be joining in the nursery rhyme.

In action rhymes like 'This is the way we wash our clothes', pause before saying 'wash' and mime washing. Get the child to do this – miming washing and saying 'wash'. Continue this game until the child is saying the word for you in the pause. You can often make up new verses in rhymes like this – e.g. 'This is the way we *eat* our meat'.

Drawing

A very good way of eliciting conversation is for mum to do a simple drawing (house, man etc.) and describe what she is doing, perhaps inventing a story. You can then bring the child into the conversation, e.g. 'What shall we put into the room?' Similarly the child can be encouraged to draw and *talk* about what he has drawn.

Dressing-up games

Dressing-up often helps to build up a pretend situation, e.g. dressing-up as the postman, conductor, etc. Then he can be encouraged to 'act out' the role (using language) with mum taking a part as well.

BOOKLET 2: ASK FOR IT

No need to talk

Learning to speak is a tremendous effort for a handicapped child. If the effort is not worthwhile he may give up, just as we do when we go abroad and discover we can get by with gestures or can find someone who understands *our* language.

A handicapped child often finds in his mum a person who understands him all too well and anticipates his every wish.

If this happens, the child does not need to talk, for he can get what he wants without speech. Indeed, the indulgent parent may positively be encouraging the child to continue using gestures or having tantrums. This is not a satisfactory way of communicating with people.

Making language worth the effort

It is important that at an early age you begin to demand some effort on the child's part before he gets what he wants.

The key to success in this is to pick on something that your child really likes so that you can be sure he will work hard to obtain it. This could be one of many things: having a sweet or a drink, being hugged or lifted up, getting a particular toy to play with or even, with severely handicapped children, simply being moved from the tummy on to the back.

The difficulty is in knowing how much you can reasonably expect and how firm you can be. If you observe your child carefully and objectively, and record what you see and hear, then you will know precisely what he *can* say – even if it is only one sound or word. It is not unreasonable to expect him to say this sound or word before he gets what he wants.

But even this may be a big effort for him – do not, at first, make demands all the time. Set aside a short time each day in which to get him to 'ask', and then gradually increase the length of time.

Snack-time

Here is an example of how you can get your child asking for things. Remember, you can adapt the basic ideas to suit your child, but here the example deals with a child who likes cake. This is what you do:

(a)   Cut up the cake into very small pieces.

(b)   Sit opposite your child at a small table; if possible, so that he can see your face clearly and you can quickly and easily give him food and control the situation.

(c)   Have ready a small portion of cake and hold it up near your face.

(d)   Encourage your child to look at you. *Immediately* he looks at you (and at the cake) pop it into his mouth. Do this until he has got the idea and *looks* at you every time he is ready for another helping.

(e)   The next step is to encourage your child to look at you *and* make a sound. Copy him by making one of *his* sounds and gradually stop giving him cake until he has looked at you and made a sound but do not count crying or tantrums (if this happens ignore him, turn away etc.). *Immediately* he looks in your direction and utters a sound – pop the cake in his mouth and praise him. Go on, until he has the idea and nearly always 'asks' for food.

(f)   Listen carefully to the sounds your child can make. One may sound a little like a word. For instance, 'gigi' sounds a little like 'Give me' or 'Gimme'. Every time your child makes *this* sound, give him the cake; praise him and repeat the word 'Give me' or 'Gimme'. Gradually stop rewarding the other sounds he makes and reward only 'Gigi'. Go on doing this until he has the idea and is saying 'Gigi' every time he 'asks'.

(g)   Continue to make tiny steps forward in this way. When

he has entirely mastered one step, go on to the next. Even at the start you will have taught your child some important lessons:

   (i)   language is worthwhile – by using it you get what you want – in this case, food.

   (ii)   you have to ask for what you want.

  (iii) in order to communicate with someone you must look at them.

Your child's preferences

You can use exactly the same procedure with all types of food: ice-cream, jelly, biscuits, nuts, orange-juice. The choice can be determined by your child's preferences.

But remember you can equally well use these ideas in other situations, e.g. the child has to 'ask' before you lift him up or throw a ball to him or push him on a swing etc. Again, you would go through the same stages as outlined in the example.

Moving further on

Although we have described the game for a child only starting to make sounds, you can use the same ideas with a child who is already speaking, in order to improve his ability to express himself. The idea is always to start with something the child can already do, and then very gradually to increase your demands, i.e. you begin by rewarding any attempt and by degrees you reward (or appear to understand) only a near approximation of the correct word or sentence.

You can help your child to build up sentences by this means. If he learns to say 'cake' before he is rewarded, you can let him finish your sentence, 'I want a . . .' with 'cake'. Gradually you leave out more of the sentence, i.e. 'I want . . .' ('a cake'), or 'I . . .' ('want a cake'), until he is using the whole sentence, 'I want a cake'. You will find further suggestions of games to play in the booklet 'Putting Two Words Together' (p. 103) and 'Ideas into Words' (p. 11).

Special toys

As well as toys which a child can get for himself, it is a good idea to keep a few special toys locked away which have to be asked for.

He will learn more quickly to ask for what he wants if you are fairly strict about this. If he says *engine* and then cries when you give it to him you may suspect he really wanted the *bus*. You should *not* quickly change the engine for the bus, but let him learn to abide by his own choice.

As he gets better at asking you could have several toys which are rather similar, so that he now has to describe the one he wants in rather more detail. For instance, you could provide several matchbox cars. If he asks for a car, you then ask which one and he must describe the car, i.e. a blue mini, etc. Again he should only get what he has asked for. Help him by asking questions such as:

Q.   How can you tell your car from Guy's car?
A.   His car has a red door.

Drawing

Most children like their parents to paint or draw for them, especially if they get a chance to dictate what should be drawn. You need not have any particular artistic talent in order to do this, a simple drawing (stick men etc.) will suffice. As you draw a house perhaps throw in questions such as:

Q.   What shall I put here?
Q.   Who sleeps in this room?
Q.   Do I need anything else at the window?
Q.   I wonder what colour the curtains should be?
Q.   Look, I've drawn one of their pets. Can you guess what it is?

Sometimes reluctant speakers can be teased into answering if the parent makes a deliberate mistake saying 'Look, I've drawn a rabbit!', when the animal is obviously a horse. This may lead to the child saying indignantly, 'It's not a rabbit, it's a horse!'

Silly questions

There is a saying, 'Silly questions get silly answers'. Yet it is all too easy to ask children silly questions. A question is surely silly if it is obvious that you do not want to know the answer.

How often, in your anxiety to get your child saying something, do you ask this kind of question? 'What's this?' (holding up an object – a shoe, a ball, etc.) 'What colour is it?' (pointing to a dress, cup, crayon, etc.) 'How many legs have I?'

If you overdo this kind of question, it soon becomes patently obvious that you do not want to know the answer, and as far as the child is concerned, nothing is gained by answering.

Lastly, try to avoid using too many questions which require only a YES or NO answer, e.g. 'Do you want a biscuit', 'Shall we go and read your book', 'Are those daddy's shoes'. Instead, try to put the question in such a way that the child has to describe what it is or what he wants. Here are some examples of more meaningful questions.

Meaningful questions

The type of question you ask must depend on your child's ability to talk. For example, if he only talks in single words, then you could use the following questions:

Q.   What do you think he's doing?
A.   Kicking or eating or sleeping etc.
Q.   What do you want to play with?
A.   Teddy or car or bike etc.

However, as your child's language develops you can start asking questions which require two or more words in the answer. Often we forget to do this and are content to accept one-word answers from the child. You can ask questions such as:

Q.   What is happening in this picture?
A.   Boy kicking.
Q.   What's he doing?
A.   Baby eating.

And so on to longer and more complex answers, for instance:

Q.   What will he do now?

A.   Teddy go to shops.

All these stages come before grammatically correct sentences, but you can encourage these at the right time.

Q.   What other toys do you think he has got?

A.   He's got a car and an engine.

Choice

If we want to make answering questions worthwhile we should give our children some choice in the matter. This immediately makes the questions meaningful. Here are some examples:

Q.   Which toy would you like to play with?

Q.   Which dress are you going to wear today?

Q.   What would you like to drink?

It is most important to abide by the child's choice once it has been given to him. To begin with it is best to give only two alternatives:

Q.   Would you like tea or coffee?

Q.   Do you want to wear the green dress or the blue one?

You should give your child the one he chooses, even if you suspect that he does not fully understand the choice. In this way he will learn to understand quite quickly and will see the point of asking.

Tell me

Here are some picture games to play with your child. First, prepare a set of folded cards with a different picture on each one, e.g. *Set 1*: A picture of a man, a house, a tent, a caravan, a castle, a block of flats, a palace etc. (see Figure 25). You could also use Galt's 'Find it Lotto' for this game.

This game can be played either with one child or several children, and can be made into a competition if you wish.

This is how to play:

Lay the pictures of houses etc. in a row in front of you but give each child a picture of a man.

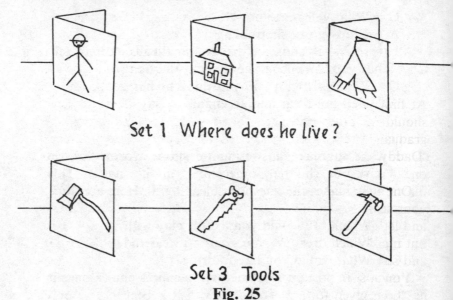

Set 1   Where does he live?

Set 3   Tools
Fig. 25

Then ask (pointing to the man), 'This is Daddy. Tell me, where does Daddy live?'

The child has to point to a picture and say: 'Daddy lives in a . . .'.

When he has answered correctly, he is given the card with the appropriate picture. If he is wrong, tell him the correct answer but leave the card in its place.

The idea is to collect as many cards as possible.

There are many variations to this game. You could turn the cards round so that the child can only see the back – so introduce an element of chance.

Various sets of material can be provided.

Set 2   A picture of a man. A shoe-shop. A greengrocer's. A post office.

A fish shop. An office. A fire station. A farm. etc.

The question then is:

Q.   Where is Daddy going today?

A.   Daddy is going to the fire station.

Set 3   A man. A hammer. A chisel. A saw. Nails. A pair of
          pliers, etc. (see Figure 25).
     Q.   What is Daddy going to use to knock nails in?
     A.   Daddy is going to use the hammer, or Daddy is
          going to use a hammer to knock the nails in.

At first your child may only be able to say 'hammer' and
should be given the card for this answer. He should be
gradually encouraged to form a sentence, i.e. 'use hammer',
'Daddy use hammer', 'Daddy going to use hammer' and so
on.

One way of encouraging him is by letting him finish off
your sentence. You might say 'Daddy is going to use a . . .'
and let him fill in the word 'hammer'. Then, gradually, leave
out more words, i.e. 'Daddy is going to . . .', 'use a hammer'
and so on.

You will be able to think of many variations of this game.

BOOKLET 3: TALKING TOGETHER

At first, very young or immature children do not really play together or talk to one another. They may play happily side by side but each child is involved in his own game. Similarly, while two children may appear to be carrying on a conversation, they are not really doing so. They do not answer each other's questions and find it difficult to wait for a turn to speak – often they both try to speak at once.

When children do start playing together, it is in games which demand very little verbal communication. They may chase one another; or play ball; or hide and seek, but often drop out or spoil the game when it involves following simple spoken rules, such as: 'you're out' or 'it's not your turn'.

Similarly, when playing with toys they will just take the one they want, and fights may ensue. They cannot, as yet put their desires into words, e.g. 'Please may I play with the train?' or 'It's mine!'

Often we protect a handicapped child by allowing him to have a toy without asking, or by not insisting that he sticks to the rules of the game.

This may be false kindness in the long run. It is important that your child should be able to play with his peers and be accepted by them. If he cannot take turns or obey the rules other children will sooner or later stop playing with him because he 'spoils the game'.

This booklet describes some games to play which should help your child to learn to play with others. We also suggest games which will help him to talk to other children and co-operate with them, once he has got to the point of joining in with a group.

However, some of these games are quite difficult and are designed for children who are already talking rather than for very young or immature children. With younger children you should start by getting them to play a simple game with one other child, or to join in a nursery rhyme or game without words where they can learn to take turns. Only introduce the harder games very gradually. If your child is an older child, although you may play with him by yourself sometimes, it is also important to try to persuade some neighbours' children or friends to join in.

Playing together

The first step towards social communication is to get children playing together in games which demand some co-operation. A shy child will start to play with one partner before joining a larger group.

The following games are useful for getting two or more children to co-operate: throwing and catching balls, playing on a see-saw, pushing one another on a swing, hide and seek, three-legged races, wheelbarrow races and tug-of-war, chasing games etc.

Indoor games with rules

Children learn to co-operate and take turns when they play race games together. The games you buy in the shops are often far too difficult for a handicapped child to play straight away. However, he *can* be taught the rules if you start with a simpler version. Here are some examples:

Race Game

Prepare a simple board like that in Figure 26. Make a dice with a small wooden brick but instead of the pips, paint the sides alternately red and green. Children take turns to throw the dice. If it falls on a green side, the player moves forward one space. If the red side is uppermost, he must wait a turn. Have a small sweet etc. as a prize. When the child can play this game well, you can introduce two pips on one of the green sides and teach him to move forward two spaces and so

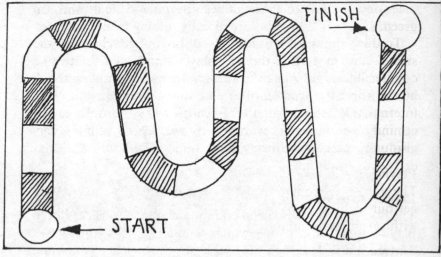

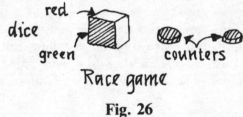

Race game

Fig. 26

on, until eventually he can play conventional race games with dice. You can gradually add other rules, one at a time – such as that when a player lands on a certain square he must go back two spaces, etc. (You can paint two pips on the board so that the child knows what to do.) In this way you can teach many different games by taking a step at a time.

Simple snakes and ladders
With the conventional game a child has many different concepts to master. He could probably master these one at a time but not all together. One concept is – if you land at the bottom of a ladder, go up – if you are at the top of a snake, come down.

As before, this can be played with a simple red and green

dice, once he has the idea of waiting on red and going on green.

To this you are adding 'up on the ladder' and 'down on the snake'. You can all chant 'Up the ladder!' when the child's counter lands at the bottom of a ladder or 'Down the snake!' at the top of a snake. After a while your child will have internalised these instructions and you will no longer need to remind him. When he can play a simple version of the game, gradually introduce other rules.

Playing and talking together
The games above have been mostly silent. Now we need to get our child to join in games with words, and also to play with several other children.

The red, red sea
An area of a room or yard is the 'red, red sea' with areas of dry land on either side and a semi-circle for a 'den' (see Figure 27).

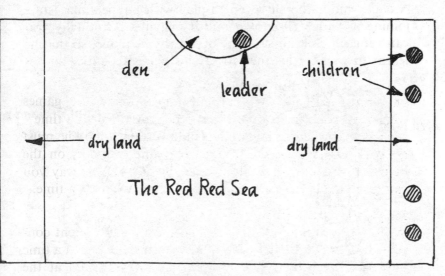

The Red Red Sea
Fig. 27

The leader stands in the den and chants, 'You can't get across the red, red sea unless ...'. Then he adds some qualifying remark like '... unless you have brown shoes, or wear glasses or have a blue pullover etc.' Then only those with the brown shoes etc. are allowed to run across to the other side and the rest try not to be caught by the leader. Anyone who is caught has to stand out. The last child to be caught becomes the next leader.

Glove puppets
One way of breaking the ice among a group of children is to give each of them a glove puppet. A shy child often starts talking to the other children, by speaking for his puppet: when he is playing a role he feels less self-conscious than when he is being himself. These puppets do not need to be elaborate and can be made from old socks: sew on buttons for the eyes, a piece of felt for the mouth etc. (see Figure 28).

Nursery rhyme games
A child who is too shy even to play with puppets may start in with well-known nursery rhymes. Gradually you each child to say part of the rhyme alone, so that he to wait for his turn to say his part. Repetitive stories

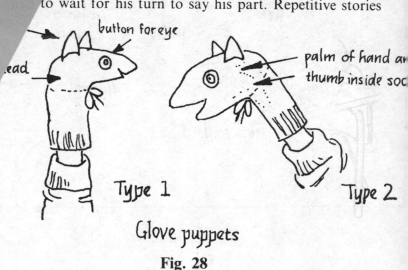

Glove puppets

Fig. 28

can also be used, like 'The Little Red Hen' or 'The Gingerbread Man'. A grown-up can tell the story, but let the children join in the repetitive part like 'Run, run as fast as you can, you can't catch me, I'm the Gingerbread man'. When your child is used to joining in with the others, you can let him say the rhyme by himself, or take a part.

Games for two children

These games help children to describe carefully what they see, or what they are doing, to another child who cannot see them. These are quiet, sitting-down games with two children at a table, and a screen of some kind between them, so that they cannot see one another. A large sheet of card or a curtain will do. There should be an opening in the screen, so that cards can be passed from child to child (see Figure 29).

Screen with children on either side

table

Fig. 29

To begin with, a grown-up may have to take the part of the second child in these games. Later he may have to act as *referee* and stand by to help out when required. However, the aim is to get two children to play the game on their own.

Drawing game

Each child has several sheets of paper and a tin of coloured crayons in front of him. The children take turns in being the 'teacher'. The 'teacher' has to tell the 'pupil' what to draw. For instance, he tells the pupil to draw a red circle. When the pupil has drawn it he posts it back to the teacher. The teacher looks at it and comments, i.e. 'That's very good!' or 'That's not a red circle, it's a *blue* circle' or 'That's not a circle, it's just a scribble!'. He then instructs the pupil again until he is satisfied.

Even if a child's drawing is poor, he can play this game – if he can draw a line or even 'scribble' a bit he can be told what colour to use.

Ring-a-picture

A useful variation of the drawing game. You need two identical pictures with plenty of detail of objects and people. Each child needs a pencil or crayon. This time the picture gets posted back and forth quite often. The teacher has a wide choice of possible 'instructions'. He may say, 'Draw a ring around the elephant's tail', or 'Draw a cross on the bicycle' etc.

When he sees what the other child has done he may say, 'I said a *ring* around the elephant's tail. You have put a *cross* – do it again.' Of course, many children will find it hard to express themselves as well as this and may only be able to say, 'ring wrong!', but this game will help them to learn to express themselves.

What is it?

This time each child either has a collection of identical toys in front of him or six cards with pictures of common objects on them. The 'teacher' this time has to describe one of the pictures or objects *without* naming it (children may need help in doing this at first), e.g. 'It catches mice', or 'It is round and bouncy!' The 'pupil' must point to the object on his side and also *name* it aloud. The 'teacher' then says, 'Yes, that's right, it's a cat', or 'No, it's not a cup, it's round and bouncy and you can catch it'.

Another version of this game is to use pictures of actions (e.g. children dancing, eating, sleeping etc.) instead of objects.

Porthole pictures
For this game you need a sheet of card with identical pictures pasted on either side. Make sure the pictures are carefully lined up (see Figure 30). Holes should be pierced in the card in strategic positions, big enough for a pencil to be passed

Porthole Pictures

Fig. 30

through. The 'teacher' says, 'Show me the duck on the pond'. The pupil then sticks his pencil through the hole so that the teacher can see it and tell him if he is right, or get him to try again. Children take turns in being teacher!

Dressing the doll

For this game each child has a cardboard doll and an identical set of paper clothes that fit on to it (see Figure 31). (These can often be bought from toy shops or book shops.) One child tells the other how to dress the doll: 'First, put on his green shirt and then his green jersey and red cap' and so on.

Dressing the doll

Fig. 31

Mothers and fathers

For this you need pictures of spoons, forks, saucepans, hammers, saws etc. One child decides to be 'mother' or 'father' and to describe what he is going to do. He says something like this, 'I am going out to dig the garden. Please give me the tool I shall need.' The other looks at his tools and says, 'You will need a garden fork', and finds the picture of the garden fork. If it is wrong, the first child will correct the other one saying, 'That's not a garden fork, it's a kitchen fork'. This game can be played with or without a screen.

Who knows?

Several children can play this game. You will need a collection of pictures on small cards. Each player has a large card marked out in squares to hold six or more of the small pictures. The question-master takes one card from the pack and without showing it to the other children must describe it, e.g. 'It's a toy and is yellow and furry'. The first to guess what it is ... i.e. 'It's a teddy bear', gets the picture to put on their card. The first child to fill a card wins the game and gets a sweet or star as a prize.

To start with you will probably have to help your child to take his turn in being a question-master until he understands what he has to do.

Phone-a-message
For this game ideally you need toy telephones which work, or, for novelty, two tins joined by a long string (see Figure 32). Two children are in adjoining rooms with a phone in each.

One child rings the other and gives him instructions to bring something. The second child then puts the phone down and delivers the goods. He then goes back to his room and it is his turn to give instructions to the other messenger.

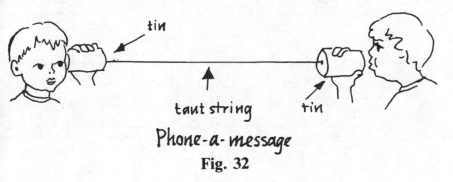

tin

taut string   tin

Phone-a-message
Fig. 32

SECTION 4: LANGUAGE AND THINKING

Introduction

INTRODUCTION

Thus far in the book, we have been concentrating on language as a means of communication. But one other important use of language is as an aid to thinking.

In this section we shall be concentrating on three aspects of thinking where language is particularly important. The first booklet deals with the use of language in remembering, and the emphasis is on memory games.

The second booklet is concerned with 'organising the world'. That is, learning to group objects and developing concepts of colour, size etc.

The third booklet deals with the development of 'inner-language': the ability to talk to ourselves. Language is particularly important in self-direction and the games in this booklet are designed with this in mind.

You will probably find this section particularly useful if your child has mastered all the basic language skills, although some of the games could be used with children whose language is still immature, e.g. speaking in two- or three-word sentences.

BOOKLET 1: TRY TO REMEMBER

This booklet is concerned with remembering – something that we all have to do, although some of us are better at it than others. We rely a great deal on our ability to remember, for instance, in finding our way back home from the shops, remembering where the shops are in the first place and what we went to the shops for! Here we are remembering how to do things. We also use our memories to relive past events, and this is where language becomes important; for language is often the means we use to recall the past, e.g. telling others about what happened on holiday or what a person looks like.

But, both in remembering how to do things, and recalling past events, we cannot remember if the information has not gone in, in the first place. The ability to take in information is just as important a part of memory as is recalling the information. These two aspects of memory – taking in and recalling information – are something that we have learnt to do through practice. However, handicapped children often have difficulty in taking in information and consequently they have difficulty in remembering. The games in this booklet can be used to give children practice at taking information in and recalling it. With all these games, remember that we often take in information much better if it is presented clearly and in an exciting and interesting way.

Everyday activities
Before taking the child on an outing, talk about what you are going to do: 'we're going to post this letter, buy a stamp, lick it, put it on the letter'.

At first you should do this just before the outing, but later you can do the preparation the day before. This will also help your child to get an idea of time.

By going over an event in this manner, you will be helping your child to take in the information during the outing, and also making him a more active participant.

When you return home you can relive the activity by making a scrap-book, or by using models or playing a pretend game. With all these activities, the child will be reliving and remembering the outing.

Special treats
You can play the same sort of game before and after some special event, like going on a train, a birthday party, bonfire night etc. Talk about what will happen beforehand – perhaps using pictures, and then relive the occasion by making a scrap-book of souvenirs, or by playing a pretend game.

Story books
You can also use story books to help your child to remember. One way is simply to have your child tell you the story (or part of the story) while looking at the pictures.

Alternatively, if you have a second copy of the same story book, you can cut out the pictures and paste them on to separate pieces of card. You can then mix them up, so that your child has to put them into the right order before telling the story. This ensures that the child really does remember the story. You could use E.S.A.'s 'Look and Find the Story' for this.

Posting-box
Make a hole in a cardboard box and place it upside down (see p. 83). Collect together about ten fairly small toys or objects that you know the child can name. Start off with only two or three. Drop them into the box one at a time, getting the child to name them before they go in. Once they are all in the box, ask the child to remember them – then lift up the box to see if he has forgotten any. It is also worth giving him some clues if he can't remember an object, e.g. 'What was

there for eating with?' or 'What blue thing was there?' In this way you will be helping the child to remember.

Alternatively, you could use a posting-box with a false bottom (see p. 84). Here you can let him pull back the false bottom to make the objects re-appear, once he has remembered all of them.

Incidentally you can easily make this into a competition to see who can remember the most.

Spot the picture

Paste some pictures of objects on to postcards; one picture per card. It is important for this game that the backs of all the cards are identical. Start the game using only two or three pictures. Show the child a picture and have him name it, then place it face down on the table. Show him the next picture, have him name it then place it face down beside the first one and so on until all the cards are face down on the table. Then say 'find me the . . .' (name one of the pictures). If he gets it right, give him a sweet or else keep a score. If he's not right first time, lift the cards, shuffle them and have another go. (By the way, children usually remember best the first or last pictures, so if you want to make it easy, call out one of these.) You can make the game harder by increasing the number of pictures included, but ten is probably the maximum to use.

You can help the child remember, if instead of naming each card by itself, you also get him to repeat the names of the pictures that have gone before. Incidentally, this is a good game for two to play. It can be two children, each taking it in turn to deal the cards or to remember. The one with the most points being the winner. But even mum and dad should take a turn at remembering, for the dealer (the child) also has to remember the name of the picture to be remembered. So this is a memory game for the child even if he's dealing the cards and mum is remembering.

Kim's game

Place a number of small objects on a tray, making sure your child can name all of them. At first, start with three or four objects but you could gradually build up to fifteen. Let him look at them for a minute or so, then cover the tray and take away some of the objects. (You can vary the number from just one object, to all of them, thus giving a surprise element to the game.) Uncover the tray and show the child the remaining objects and say, 'What have I taken away?' As in the previous game, you can give him clues to the objects he has forgotten.

You can also use this game to help your child 'take in' the names of objects present. Do this by having him sort the objects into groups while he is looking at them, e.g. say 'Let's put all the things for eating with in this corner; all the toys here' etc. Have only three or four objects in each group at the most.

Incidentally, this game can also be played using pictures rather than objects, so that you could make sure the objects can be sorted into neat groups by having pictures of animals, items of clothing, things to eat etc.

Sorting it out

Another variation of the previous game is to show the child a picture on which there are many different objects. Let him look at it for a while, then take it away and ask him to remember all the things he saw. As before, you can help him take in the information by saying 'Look at all the animals', or 'What furniture is there?' or 'Who are the people?'. When it comes to remembering, you can say, 'Tell me all the animals you saw'.

Fetching game

Scatter a variety of objects (or pictures of objects) around the floor and then give your child a 'shopping list', e.g. 'I want you to bring me a ball, cup, dog' (naming a selection of the objects).

Start off with just a few but you gradually increase the list. Give points (exchangeable for a sweet perhaps) for those brought that you have asked for and subtract points for wrong ones.

Give away
This is a variation on the previous game except this time the child has to give things out. Put some objects (or pictures of objects) into a box or basket and then give the child instructions about what he has to do with each, e.g. 'Give the ball to daddy, put the cup on the settee and the pen under the large chair in the hall'. You can then give him points for the number he gets right.

The game can be made more difficult by increasing the number of instructions.

BOOKLET 2: SORTING IT OUT

How many animals can you think of that are small, white and furry? But in case you spend too much time in answering the question, we should say that our main reason for asking it is to show how we use language to group things together, e.g. the word 'animal' refers to a large group of living things, ranging from ant to zebra. While in a group of white things we could include rats, snow and paper.

Every day we are continually grouping things: when we talk of the *red* coat we saw in a *large* store, we are describing the coat and the store in terms of the groups they come in, e.g. the coat goes into the group of red things. This not only helps us to communicate more precisely with other people (a *red* coat not a yellow or blue one) but it is a way of organising our past experience and is an aid in thinking.

The ability to group or see relationships between things is one of the most important abilities that children have to learn, yet it is not easy for them. For instance, we consider a post box and a fire engine are alike in that both are 'red' yet they are completely different both in size and shape. This is where the difficulty starts for children. Objects can vary in so many ways – size, colour, shape, feel, to mention only a few – that children find it difficult to pick out the one feature which objects have in common and that enables us to say they are alike. What children have to learn to do is to find the features objects have in common and ignore all others. To make it easier for the child it is best to start by concentrating on obvious groupings such as colour and size before moving on to groupings based on shape or feel. But it is vitally important that you do move on to these, for features like shape are not particularly noticeable and if you concentrate only on the more obvious features, like colour, the child will never learn that shape is another important basis for grouping objects.

Likewise, you can also introduce fairly early on groupings based on a common function, e.g. things for eating, playing with or wearing. Later on will come the more abstract groupings of animals, furniture etc.

The games in this booklet are designed to help children learn the various ways in which objects can be grouped. Remember that you can often use the same game to teach different groupings, e.g. initially you might use the Sorting Games to teach colour but you can later use them for teaching shape.

However, even when you are concentrating on one type of grouping, it is important to start the game off in a very simple way, so that the child grasps the idea before making the game more complex. An example of how you can do this is given in the Post-Box Game, but you can do the same thing with all the games mentioned.

Finally, once your child begins to group the objects correctly, you can start teaching the words we use to describe the feature the objects have in common, i.e. they are 'red', or 'small' or 'animals'.

Sorting games

Having the child sort objects or pictures of objects into groups is a very good way of helping him learn why things belong together. You can use almost anything in these games, e.g. with a 'toy' farm you could have him put all the *animals* in one field, the *things for driving* in another, the *buildings* in a third. Or you could have him sort buttons into various colours or into sizes. You could also use pictures of objects – and have him sort these.

You can make sorting games more exciting if you turn them into a competition between you and the child or between children, with a prize for the winner (either the fastest or the one with the least mistakes).

You can also complicate the game, having the child sort the items one way, then asking him to sort the items a different way, e.g. with buttons he could sort first by colour, then by size.

Even harder is sorting simultaneously by colour and size. Instead of having just two piles the child now has to sort into four or more piles, i.e. large black, large white, small black and small white.

Fetching games

Another sorting game that is particularly suitable for the energetic child involves fetching things. Scatter some objects or pictures of objects around the room (or garden). Show the child an object and ask him to bring you another that's the same colour (or shape etc.) or that has the same use (e.g. for eating with). If he brings the right one, make a great fuss, but if it's wrong don't take it from him but tell him to find another. As before, in this game the child is having to sort through objects until he finds the right ones.

You can also turn the game into a competition between children to see who collects all the objects first. But mum and dad can also take a turn at collecting the objects and asking the child if it's right (a few deliberate mistakes will keep him interested).

Scrap-books

Alongside the sorting games, it is useful to make a scrap-book containing groups of pictures. Each scrap-book could be for a different grouping, e.g. a colour book or size book. On each page have a collection of objects all of the same size, e.g. big objects on one page, little objects on another etc. (see Figure 33). Start with only one or two objects per page, so that through time your child can add other pictures. (Old catalogues are a useful source of pictures.) Also you can help your child realise that the same object can occur in a variety of groups, by having an identical picture in several different groupings, e.g. a picture of a red ball could be in with red things, toys and 'round' things.

Scrap-book — little and big
Fig. 33

When you have a collection of objects on each page you can weave a story around the pictures, perhaps getting your child to take part by saying the word that describes the group, e.g. 'One day the boy wearing the *green* jumper went for a drive in his dad's *green* car. He saw a tree with *green* leaves and a *green* snake in the *green* grass.'

Pictures
When looking at pictures that show a lot of different things (e.g. wall pictures) you can ask your child to point out all the 'red things', 'all the people' or 'things for eating'.

Equally, encourage your child to tell *you* what to point out. This will give him practice at using words like 'animal', 'red' etc., and once again you can always make a mistake and have him correct you!

I Spy

Another way of using pictures which show plenty of objects is to have a game of *I Spy*, but instead of using letters, describe a feature of the object, e.g. 'I spy with my little eye something that is round' (or red or an animal etc.). Again, the child should take a turn at saying 'I spy . . .'.

This is also a game that you can use anywhere – around the house, in the car or when walking outside. It is also good to give your child other clues if he's not successful in guessing, e.g. if it's I Spy an animal, you can then add . . . it's large . . . it's brown . . . you ride on it.

Likewise if you're doing the guessing, ask him to give you this sort of clue.

Posting-box

This game is a little more difficult than the previous one, for here the child has to remember the features the objects have in common when he is sorting. Hence you could begin using this game when your child has started to sort the objects correctly.

Start off with a simple box (see p. 83) but later make a posting-box with sliding lids (see p. 84) out of cardboard or wood. Collect together a number of objects, some of which are alike in some way (e.g. the same colour) and others which are different. Ask your child to put all the red ones in the box and show him an example of a red object. You can then compare his choice with the sample, but only pull back the top lid to let the object go in if it is a red object. If not, encourage him to try another. When all the red ones are in the box, you (or the child) can pull back the bottom to make them re-appear, saying 'look at all the *red* things'. Repeat the game until the child can do it without any mistakes.

This game can start off very simply but you easily make it more difficult. Here are some ideas:

(a)   Although you may have only two or three objects in each group at the beginning, gradually increase the number of objects. Indeed, you can test whether your child has grasped the idea of 'redness' by noting if he immediately groups new objects correctly.

(b)   Start with only two groups of objects but then gradually add other groupings, e.g. have only red and green at the beginning then add blue, yellow etc.

(c)   Once your child has grasped the idea of grouping you can start concentrating on getting him to use the words which describe the grouping, e.g., before he is allowed to post the object he has to say '*red* bus' or '*red* hat'. Then before all the objects re-appear, he has to say '*red*'.

(d)   Later on, when your child can sort the items easily, you can introduce what's called 'cross classification'. On one occasion ask him to post the red things. When he has done that, change the grouping to something else, e.g. soft ones, but still use the same objects.

It is quite difficult for the child to change the grouping, so don't introduce this until you are sure he can sort the items by both colour and feel.

Treasure Hunt
This is a game you can play indoors using either actual objects or pictures of objects. But you can also play it outside in the garden, park, playground or on the beach. The idea is to give your child a list of the treasures you want, e.g. something red, something soft, something that's made of wood, something flat etc. (Incidentally, this is a good memory game as well.) You can make this into a competition between children (handicap the more able ones by giving them a longer list).

Odd man out
Before you can identify which is the 'odd man out', you have to be able to give a reason for why the other things go together. Hence, this is a useful game to teach grouping. You can play if with pictures, e.g. have pictures of a knife, fork and balloon. If the child picks the balloon then give him a sweet or else keep a score. You can keep the child's interest if you place the pictures in front of a box under which a sweet

can be hidden. He can then lift the box to see if the sweet's there. Start off with easy groupings (e.g. two red cards and a blue one) then make it more difficult.

Happy families

A variation of this well known game can be a good way of teaching grouping. Instead of families made up of people, have 'families' of things for eating; for wearing; for driving etc. but the idea is basically the same. The cards are all shuffled and dealt to the players. They then swop cards with the other players to try and get a complete family. The first person to do this is the winner. You can make the game last longer by increasing the number of members of each family or by having several families per player. But initially you will have to keep the game simple until your child grasps the idea.

Picture dominoes

You can buy these at most good toy shops. Instead of numbers the dominoes (usually made of card) have two pictures. Although the idea of these dominoes is for the child to find an identical picture to match the one on the table, you can vary the game by allowing the child to put down a 'related' picture – as long as he gives a reason, e.g. if apple is on the table, then he could put down a banana (reason: 'it's for eating') or a ball (reason: 'it's round'). If he can't give a reason, then he can't put it down (see Figure 34).

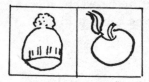 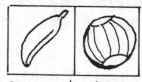 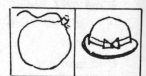

Picture dominoes
Fig. 34

Category snap

The same idea can be used for a variation of the game 'snap'. This time however there are no identical cards in the pack, but the person can call SNAP if the cards are related in some way, e.g. they are both animals, or both the same colour; but he has to say why he called SNAP. To make your own cards, cut out pictures from magazines or catalogues and paste them on to cards. Start off with a small number of cards until your child gets the idea.

Gradually make the game more difficult by introducing new cards and different groupings. You can also eliminate the more obvious ones (e.g. colour) either by using black and white drawings or by making a rule of 'no colours' allowed.

Hunt the thimble

This can be played in the usual manner – a thimble (or a bar of chocolate to make the game more exciting) is hidden somewhere. The child then has to find it, but you can give him clues, e.g. it's under something *soft* . . . and *red* . . . *for sitting on* etc.

Equally, if he hides something, ask him for similar clues.

Around the house

You can often get the child to do little jobs around the house that will require him to sort things out, e.g. 'Bring me the *big* potatoes for chips' or 'Put the tins into one cupboard, the packets in the other'. The children can also sort their toys out – all the cars go into one box; the toy soldiers another box. Or they can sort their books into large ones, small ones etc. and have them on different shelves.

Final thoughts

As we said at the beginning, children can find learning to group objects very difficult. Not only do they need plenty of practice (lots of different games) but we also need to provide them with lots of examples of things that go together. Otherwise they will not really learn what the concepts 'red', 'large', 'animal' etc. mean.

Do not be too discouraged if the child makes lots of mistakes during the games. Indeed, you can learn a lot by noting the type of mistakes he makes, e.g. you want your child to group objects by shape and show him a red ball and say

'Give me one like this'. If he gives you a red box instead of a green ball, this is a mistake as far as you are concerned, but yet in another way – he was right (both were red). Hence the mistakes may be good mistakes. But you have to be careful not to confuse your child. If need be, change the game so that 'good' mistakes can't occur (at least in the early stages of learning a new grouping), e.g. in the above example, have all the objects the same colour and size.

BOOKLET 3: TELLING YOURSELF

Most of us talk to ourselves sometimes and may be ashamed of being caught in the act. Have you thought what it would be like if you were not able to talk to yourself?

It would be difficult to remember directions if you could not put them into words – i.e. turn right at the traffic lights, then take the first turning on the left . . . and so on.

Similarly it would be hard to organise your shopping or plan your day, if you could not put it into words.

This inner language (telling yourself) is closely akin to thought and may be spoken aloud or (more frequently) be silent.

In order to become independent, a child needs to be able to tell himself what to do, i.e. to direct himself.

Self-direction

Children learn eventually to direct themselves by first learning to do what *you* tell them.

You start helping your child in this way very early – even before he can speak. You teach him to bring you a toy by holding out your hands and at the same time saying 'car', for instance. At first the car should be not only the nearest toy but also the only toy available, so that the task is very easy. Later you can make it more difficult by getting him to choose between two toys. You will find a more detailed description of this stage in the booklet 'What's it Called?' where a fetching game is described (see p. 82).

If he has passed this stage and can bring objects from another room when you ask him, here are some more games to play which will help him to follow instructions.

Do this!

This game can be played with several children together, but it is best rehearsed with your child on his own until he is used to it. Either play some music (play the piano or put on a record) or use a whistle. Let your child run around freely. When the music stops or the whistle blows, he must stop, and then you command 'Sit down!' or 'Touch the wall!' or 'Stand on one leg!' and so on. Make these commands very simple at first. When he can play this game on his own, it is as well to bring other children in. Later more rules can be introduced – for instance, the last to follow a command must stand out.

Don't do this!

Many children are thought to be disobedient because they do not understand the negative. This is natural – children at first attend to only some of the words you say. When you say, 'Fetch the ball!' and your child brings it back, it may be that he has only really 'heard' the word 'ball'.

When you say to him, 'Don't kick the table!' your child may have only understood 'kick the table!' and may continue to do it. This is not always disobedience; it is something your child needs to learn. You can help him by varying the game of 'Do this!' by introducing negative commands. Sometimes, instead of saying, 'Touch the wall!' you call out, 'Don't touch the wall!' (and child who touches it loses a point).

You will find that it is not only handicapped children who find this difficult – most children find it much easier to *do* something than to stop themselves from doing it. Obviously it is important to be able to stop oneself and say 'no!'. Otherwise one is at the mercy of every distraction. Here are some games to help your child to stop.

No more

Give your child a jar or box and a tray of beans, and see how quickly he can fill the jar, or fill it up to a mark. When he has practised this tell him that after a minute you are going to call out 'Stop!' and he must stop at once. If he fails to stop he forfeits four or five beans. Count the beans in the jar each time and see if he can break his own record. Show your pleasure if he does well, so that even if he cannot count, he will experience success. Later you could make this game into a competition among a group of children. If you feel energetic you can work out a system of handicaps – the slowest children are given some beans in their jars before they start. This is a good idea, as a game can become frustrating if it is always the same person who wins.

What's not
Scatter small objects over the floor not too near together. Say, 'Find me something which is *not* red'. 'Find one that is *not* an animal!' and so on. For each correct find give him a counter, and see how many he can collect. You can swop these counters for a sweet at the end of the game if you like. You can play the same game with pictures. When he brings the right picture say, 'Good, that is *not* red, it's blue', or 'Good, that is *not* an animal, it's a car'.

Stop! Wait! Go!
Cut out three circles of card about 6 ins in diameter and colour them red, amber and green, and fasten each to the end of a bamboo stick or stiff wire. If possible, mark out roads on the floor or garden and let the children pretend to be cars or buses. From time to time when you see your child approaching hold out the red 'light' and shout 'STOP!'. At first you may have to put your hand out to make sure he *does* stop. He must then wait while you change to the amber 'light' (you should also say 'wait') and he may go only when you change the light to green and say 'go'.

At first you should always use the words – 'stop', 'wait', 'go' – as well as the coloured 'lights'. Later you can use the 'lights' on their own. He will then have to tell himself – stop, wait, go. (A torch with different coloured lights could be used.)

On your marks!
This is a quieter game to play indoors. Give your child a toy car. Prepare a sloping board and have a torch with a red and

green light. Tell him that when the green light flashes he can let go of the car and start the race, but not when the red light flashes. You will probably find he will let go whatever colour he sees. Let him gain a counter each time he does it correctly. If he finds this difficult say 'Green, go!' each time you flash a green light and 'Red, don't go!' to a red light. Later teach him to say 'Green, go!' 'Red, don't go!' to himself. This game should show you how much easier it is for your child to control his immediate reactions when he can direct himself with words.

Household tasks

When we are cooking a new recipe, we often have a cookery book in front of us. This tells us how to order the task – when to add the thickening, how long we should let it simmer and so on. Being able to do this for ourselves makes us independent of other people. As children get older it is important that they should be as socially independent as possible. We should encourage them to make their own beds, clean their shoes, lay the table, wash the dishes and so on. And in teaching the child these tasks, it is a good idea to use pictures of the different stages involved, as an aid to structuring the task, much as we use our cookery books. Here are some examples of ways in which pictures may be used to help children to learn to order their own tasks.

Shoe cleaning

It is important to think carefully about the stages involved in each task. For example, in shoe cleaning, these might be:
1. Put paper on the floor.
2. Remove shoes.
3. Get out cleaning box.
4. Remove mud with hard brush.
5. Apply polish.
6. Polish off with soft brush.
7. Put brushes away in box.
8. Remove paper and place in dust bin.
9. Put on shoes.

Prepare a picture to show each of these stages. You could either use pictures taken from magazines, or have a go at drawing them yourself. Rather than have the pictures lying flat on a table, why not use a magnet or flannel board to display them? Simply back your pictures with stiff card (for use on the magnet board) or with a piece of cloth (for use on the flannel board). In this way, the child can easily refer to the pictures while carrying out the task. Here is a suggested play:

(a)   Put the first three pictures in order on the board, explaining as you go; 'First put down the paper and then take off your shoes and then get out the cleaning box.'

(b)   Take down the pictures and mix them up.

(c)   Get your child to put the pictures back in order.

(d)   Carry on in this way – when your child can put three pictures in order give him another picture and show him where it goes. In this way build up to nine pictures.

These pictures will not only help your child to sort but also to name each stage of his task, i.e. as he puts a picture on the board you encourage him by saying, 'Yes, take off your shoes!'

When he has rehearsed with the pictures, let him carry out the job of cleaning his own shoes. You need not wait until he can sort all the pictures. As soon as he can sort a few pictures, he should be encouraged to start the job of shoe cleaning, even if you have to finish it at first. If he forgets what to do, instead of telling him, encourage him to use the pictures as a reminder.

You can prepare other sets of pictures showing other household tasks.

Later you could make a scrap-book which has a page for each task. On each page, put small pictures of the stages in the task in the correct order. The child can then refer to this if he forgets how a particular task should be carried out.

Incidentally, Learning Development Aids are producing a series of picture books (Barnaby Books – Help Yourself Stories), each one dealing with a particular household task.

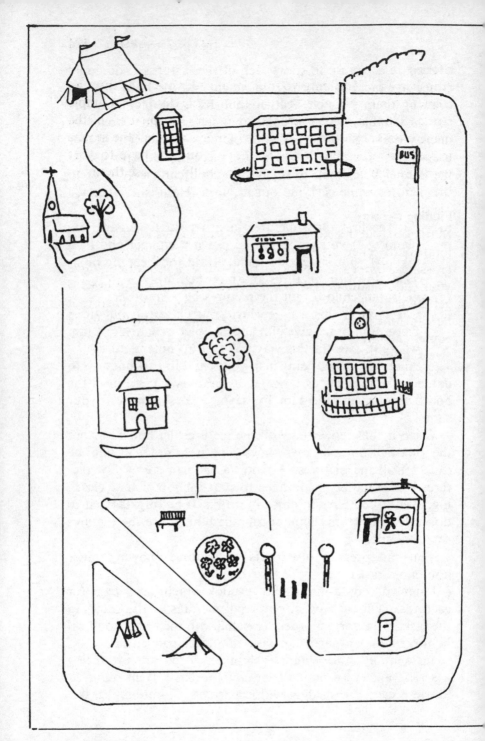

Finding the way

Fig. 35

Stories

Another way of helping your child to order events is through stories. You will probably already have told him simple stories. Choose his favourite and then cut out pictures of the main events. Let him put these in order and retell the stories to you with the help of the pictures. You may have to start with just one or two pictures and gradually increase the number.

Finding the way

Mark out on the floor, or on several sheets of paper sellotaped together, a simple imaginary map showing streets, crossings, houses, a church, a post office, a school etc. Give your child a simple task at first, such as to show you how to get from his 'house' to the shop (draw several roads so that he can find alternative routes). When he can show you the route, encourage him to describe it to you as he goes along (see Figure 35).

TOY AND BOOK SUPPLIERS

E. J. Arnold, Coal Road, Seacroft, Leeds LS14 2AE.

E.S.A. Creative Learning Ltd., Pinnacles, P.O. Box 22, Harlow, Essex CM19 5AY.

Galt Toys, Brookfield Road, Cheadle, Cheshire

Hodder & Stoughton, P.O. Box 702, Mill Road, Dunton Green, Sevenoaks, Kent TN13 2YD.

Ladybird Books, Will's & Hepworth Ltd., Loughborough, Leicestershire.

Learning Development Aids, Park Works, Norwich Road, Wisbech, Cambridge PE13 2AX.

Phillip & Tacey Ltd., North Way, Andover, Hampshire.

INDEX OF GAMES